JUNGLE
Enemies

⑤

JUNGLE DOCTOR'S
Enemies

Paul White

CF4·K

Jungle Doctor's Enemies, ISBN 978-1-84550-300-0
© Copyright 1987 Paul White
First published 1948
Reprinted 1948, 1950, 1951, 1954, 1956, 1958, 1969, 1963
Paperback edition 1972, revised edition 1987
Reprinted 1990, 1995

Published in 2007 by Christian Focus Publications,
Geanies House, Fearn, Tain, Ross-shire,
IV20 1TW, Scotland, U.K.
Paul White Productions
4/1-5 Busaco Road, Marsfield, NSW 2122, Australia

Cover design by Daniel van Straaten
Cover illustrations by Craig Howarth
Interior illustrations by Graham Wade
Printed and bound in Denmark
by Nørhaven Paperback A/S

*Since the Jungle Doctor books were first published there have been
a number of Jungle Doctors working in Mvumi Hospital, Tanzania,
East Africa - some Australian, some British, a West Indian and a
number of East African Jungle Doctors to name but a few.*

African words are used throughout the book, but explained at
least once within the text. A glossary of the more important
words is included at the front along with a key character index.

CONTENTS

Fact File: Paul White

Born in 1910 in Bowral, New South Wales, Australia, Paul had Africa in his blood for as long as he could remember. His father captured his imagination with stories of his experiences in the Boer War which left an indelible impression. His father died of meningitis in an army camp in 1915 and Paul was left an only child without his father at five years of age. He inherited his father's storytelling gift along with a mischievous sense of humour.

He committed his life to Christ as a sixteen-year-old school-boy and studied medicine as the next step towards missionary work in Africa. Paul and his wife, Mary, left Sydney, with their small son, David, for Tanganyika in 1938. He always thought of this as his life's work but Mary's severe illness forced their early return to Sydney in 1941. Their daughter, Rosemary, was born while they were overseas.

Within weeks of landing in Sydney, Paul was invited to begin a weekly radio broadcast which spread throughout Australia as the Jungle Doctor Broadcasts - the last of these was aired in 1985. The weekly scripts for these programmes became the raw material for the Jungle Doctor hospital stories - a series of twenty books.

Paul always said he preferred life to be a 'mixed grill' and so it was: writing, working as a Rheumatologist, public speaking, involvement with many Christian organisations, adapting the fable stories into multiple forms (comic books, audio cassettes, filmstrips), radio and television, sharing his love of birds with others by producing bird song cassettes - and much more...

The books in part or whole have been translated into 107 languages.

Paul saw that although his plan to work in Africa for life was turned on its head, in God's better planning he was able to reach more people by coming home than by staying. It was a great joy to meet people over the years who told him they were on their way overseas to work in mission because of the books.

Paul's wife, Mary, died after a long illness in 1970. He married Ruth and they had the joy of working together on many new projects. He died in 1992 but the stories and fables continue to attract an enthusiastic readership of all ages.

Fact file: Tanzania

The Jungle Doctor books are based on Paul White's missionary experiences in Tanzania. Today many countries in Africa have gained their independence. This has resulted in a series of name changes. Tanganyika is one such country that has now changed its name to Tanzania.

The name Tanganyika is no longer used formally for the territory. Instead the name Tanganyika is used almost exclusively to mean the lake.

During World War I, what was then Tanganyika came under British military rule. On December 9, 1961 it became independent. In 1964, it joined with the islands of Zanzibar to form the United Republic of Tanganyika and Zanzibar, changed later in the year to the United Republic of Tanzania.

It is not only its name that has changed, this area of Africa has gone through many changes since the Jungle Doctor books were first written. Africa itself has changed. Many of the same diseases raise their heads, but treatments have advanced. However new diseases come to take their place and the work goes on.

Missions throughout Africa are often now run by African Christians and not solely by foreign nationals. There are still the same problems to overcome however. The message of the gospel thankfully never changes and brings hope to those who listen and obey. *The Jungle Doctor* books are about this work to bring health and wellbeing to Africa as well as the good news of Jesus Christ and salvation.

Fact File: Vaccination

Jungle Doctor's Enemies tells what happened in East Africa in early 1940. Antibiotics were not available in East Africa then, and it would be some time before smallpox was stamped out by world-wide vaccination. During the 1940s there were no anti-measles vaccines and Tanzania was in the middle of a war. It was difficult to transport medical supplies into the country. As a result serum for vaccination was not available.

Measles is a common disease that many recover from in the West, but epidemics are still rife in third world countries. However, in the 1980s an extensive epidemic of measles was halted when 167,000 children were immunised against the virus by a medical team organised by African Enterprise.

Sir Michael Wood, a famous East African Flying Doctor wrote: 'Preventive measures such as vaccinations must come high up the list. Not only is prevention better than cure but it is also ten times cheaper.'

Bishop Festo Kivengere summed the situation up when he said: 'Can you imagine the impact for the gospel as this help comes to thousands of families in the Lord Jesus Christ's name?'

Fact File: Characters

Let's find out about the people in the story before we start. Bwana is the Chief Doctor and the one telling the stories. Daudi is his assistant. Take a moment or two now to familiarise yourself with the names of the people you will meet in this book.

Bwana – Chief Doctor

Daudi – Deputee/assistant

Madole – a native chief

Mika – the teacher

Ndogowe – a helpful villager

Samson – Handyman

Chikoti – enemy chief

Hilda – Senior nurse

Mazengo – Chikoti's grandson

Mubofu – young blind boy

Perisi – Senior nurse

Sechelela – Senior nurse

Other hospital staff: Kefa; Mboga; Mwendwa

Fact File: Words

EXPRESSIONS THAT ADD EMPHASIS:
Eheh, Heh, Hongo, Kah, Koh, Kumbe, Yoh

Bwana - a term of respect

Dudu – insect

Heya – yes

Ilende – dried herbs

Kanisa – the cathedral

Karibu – welcome

Kwaheri – goodbye

Mulungu – Almighty God

Nzoka – a snake

Serenyenyi - measles

Sindano – a needle

Tabu sana – great trouble

Waganga – witchdoctors

Wazungu – the Europeans

Chilonda – an ulcer

Habari? – what's the news?

Hodi? – may I come in

Kabisa – completely

Kanzu – a long garment

Kaya – house

Knobkerrie - knobbed stick

Nhuti – rifle

Pangas - large knives

Shaitan – the devil

Sukuma - push

Ugali - porridge

Wandugu – relations

TANZANIAN LANGUAGES: Swahili (main language)

Chigogo (one of the 150 tribal languages)

1
A Rumour and a Blind Boy

Daudi and I walked through the hospital's hyaena-proof gate. Coming towards us was an African boy. He stumbled and nearly fell, clutching at the cornstalks growing on each side of the winding path. He steadied himself for a moment, then walked uncertainly forward.

I sprang towards him, 'What's the matter? Can I help?'

For a moment he stood silent and then exclaimed in a voice thick from crying, 'Bwana, the others will not let me help push the car because I am Mubofu, the blind one, and…' He turned and began to shuffle back the way he had come, his shoulders drooping and his hands groping in front of him.

Daudi put down the baskets of medicines and instruments he was carrying. 'Bwana, let's take him with us to Dodoma. It would bring him considerable joy.'

I nodded in agreement. As the boy turned towards us, I glimpsed his face. It bore the stamp of tragedy. Two empty eye sockets told the story of hopeless native medicine. He clutched my arm. 'Bwana, I can push, even though I live in *utitu* – the land of darkness.'

'But what if you trip over as the car moves downhill?'

'*Kah*, Bwana, I am no stranger to falling. I have no fear of a bruise. Will you not allow me to help?'

The path curved round the trunk of a huge baobab tree. He unerringly followed the centre of the track to where Samson, the hospital handyman, was cranking on an A-model Ford. A group of small boys danced up and down and chanted, '*Na vilungo gwe, na vilungo gwe* – go to it with strength!'

Samson straightened up and wiped his brow. '*Hongo*, Bwana, the battery is sleeping.'

I grinned. 'The row these *wadodo* – little people – are making should wake it, surely.'

'*Kah*, our car is not called Sukuma for nothing.' (*Sukuma* is the Swahili word for push.)

'Bwana, we'll push,' shouted the small boys, rushing forward.

'*Viswanu* – right – but you must wait for a moment till Daudi and I are ready.'

Changing from Chigogo, the language of the Central Plains of Tanzania, to English I said, 'Samson, we'll take that blind boy to Dodoma. Daudi and I think it would be a red-letter day in his life to go on safari with us. You can bring him back later on when we've caught the train.'

My African friend's reply was thoughtful. 'We can be eyes for him today and tell him all we see along the road and in the town.'

Mubofu was crouching in the shade of the mud-brick shed that was Sukuma's home. On the wall above him were three many-coloured lizards busily hunting flies. As I walked over to him he rose to his feet.

'Bwana, you'll let me help push?'

'How did you know it was I coming towards you?'

'*Hongo*.' His whole face lit up, his smile accentuating the hollows where his eyes should have been. '*Kah*, Bwana, I heard your shoes in the sand and I know no African who walks like you do.'

I whistled. 'What ears you've got!'

'Bwana, my ears have to be my eyes as well.' He put his hand on my sleeve. 'Bwana, please will you let me push?'

'No, Mubofu, I will not allow you to push.'

All the joy left his face. Before he could speak I said, 'But I wondered if perhaps you would like to come on safari with us today to Dodoma.'

'*Kah*,' exclaimed the boy, 'in the car, in Sukuma?'

'*Heya* – yes.'

'*Yoh*, Bwana, it has been my strong wish for many days to travel in a car. *Kah*!'

He proceeded to do a little dance which sent the lizards clambering up the trunk of the baobab tree. I went to collect my luggage and say my goodbyes.

As we walked back to the car I questioned Daudi. 'Tell me about Mubofu. What is his story?'

'His people are dead. He sleeps in the tribal house of his relations in a village which has no time for the ways of God. I have heard it said that they feed him only because they think he will die before long anyhow, and it is a thing of small wisdom to upset the spirits of the ancestors.'

Mubofu was running his fingers over the radiator and bonnet of the car. We wedged him into the front seat between Samson and Daudi. Letting off the hand-brake I called out, '*Alu sukuma* – come on, push!'

Slowly we moved forward under twenty-boy power. The old machine gained speed as we rolled down the stony track from the hospital. I let in the clutch. Sukuma backfired noisily. Shrieking, the children scampered away. Then the engine started and we were on the first lap of a medical safari to the top of the Great Rift Wall.

We moved cautiously down a crazily cut track running through a dry river bed.

Mubofu spoke excitedly, 'It's on the hill beyond the fourth river that I live. Do I not know this part of the road very well indeed?'

'Truly,' said Daudi, 'he travels this road as well as anybody. His feet seem to know every rock and rut.'

'It was here, Bwana, at Chibaya, that I was born. It was here that I lost my eyes.'

'How did it happen, Mubofu?'

The blind boy held up four fingers. 'It was four years ago, Bwana, when *serenyenyi* came into our village.'

I looked at Daudi. His lips framed the word measles.

'*Hongo*,' continued Mubofu, 'those were days of sorrow, Bwana. First my nose and then my eyes ran. *Ehh*, how I coughed! My *wandugu* – relations – would not let me sleep. They beat tins and shouted and shook me. "You must not sleep or you'll die," they said. Then, Bwana, my eyes became filled with pain because of the glare and the flies. When they put me inside the house the smoke of the cooking fires made my eyes worse still.'

He sat up suddenly and pointed with his chin towards a group of huts. 'There is my house. There, Bwana, is where it all happened.'

'*Kah*,' said Samson, 'how do you know we've come to your house?'

'*Kumbe*,' explained the boy, 'is my nose not awake? Shall I not know the smell of my own village?'

There was silence for a while and then he said, 'Bwana, there was pain, fiery pain. In my eyes were ulcers. But there was no-one to help me.'

Something was moving in the jungle beside the road. Samson shouted, 'Look, Bwana, *mpala*...' A buck the size of a Shetland pony sprang up from a thornbush thicket and bounded away in great leaps.

'What was it?' asked Mubofu, his hand on my shoulder.

'A beautiful buck. See, there behind it is another.'

As the words passed my lips I tried to stop them from slipping out, but the boy's face was aglow. 'I can see it, Bwana, in my mind. *Yoh*, how they jump.'

The road wound in and out through thornbush country. My thoughts were about measles, remembering that worldwide epidemics occurred every five years. Another was due shortly if the wretched disease came on schedule.

We crossed a dry riverbed which in the wet season could be a muddy torrent. 'Daudi, we must be prepared

for another measles epidemic and not let this sort of thing happen again.'

Daudi nodded, 'They don't only go blind when measles attacks. Hundreds and hundreds of children die. Behold, in our own country it is a disease of trouble and death and sorrow, especially for children.'

I looked at the pitiful face beside me and thought of the torment that small boy must have suffered. He, however, was not thinking of measles and was tense with excitement. Each stage of that journey had its own particular interest to him. He amazed me as time and again he described what we had passed. His senses were unusually quick. He sat there alert as Sukuma sputtered and skidded along the Great North Road.

We were climbing a steep hill on which cactus flourished. Immediately below was a patch of dark green mango trees growing round the sandy riverbed; amongst them were the white buildings of a large boys' school. We turned off the road and drove through a peanut garden and past a carpentry workshop where schoolboys were busy making tables.

I stopped the car in the shade of a great kikuyu tree. 'It's time for food. Later we'll drive to the railway station.'

I heard from my friend, the principal of the school, that a measles epidemic had actually started. It was way up in the north in the Sudan and Kenya. 'There's no news of it in Tanzania – yet.'

The station-master, a tall Indian, informed us that the train was six hours late. He told me of a severe epidemic in his home town, Hyderabad. It sounded suspiciously like measles to me.

Samson was pumping up Sukuma's tyres. He looked up enquiringly as I came through the station gate.

'The train is six hours late,' I told them.

Mubofu laughed. '*Hongo*, Bwana, that is good. Behold, you will have time to tell me many things about Dodoma. I will see in my mind what you see with your eyes. I have never been in a place where there are so many people.'

2
Mubofu

'Samson, would you go into the shop of Ahmed Rhemtulla and load up with rice, soap and the cement that we require for the new well? Take Mubofu with you and when I have finished our arrangements here at the station I will come over and collect him and show him part of the town.

'Yes, Bwana.' He climbed in behind the wheel and drove off. Sukuma moved down the road with Mubofu leaning out of the window open-eared to every sound that the town could provide.

I could guess that Samson was telling him all about the post office and the granite fort that had been built in the days when Tanzania was German East Africa. It took a quarter of an hour to arrange bookings for Daudi and myself to Saranda, the nearest station to the hospital at Kilimatinde where we would work for a week doing eye operations.

We crossed the railway line walking on the steel sleepers and made our way past the public well. It was thronged with water carriers who paid one cent – and there are ten cents in a shilling – for each kerosene tin full of water.

Outside the Indian shop Mubofu was sitting on a box in a corner while Samson helped load bag after bag of rice.

'*Kah*, Bwana,' exclaimed the blind boy, '*kah*, has not this place a rich smell?' He wrinkled up his nose expressively.

An Indian woman was cutting up a huge lump of sticky brown sugar. 'Would you like to taste some sugar?' I asked.

Mubofu nodded his head vigorously so I handed over a five-cent piece and received a great lump of sugar as big as my closed fist. To my disgust there was a huge cockroach embalmed in it.

'*Kah*, Mubofu, there's a *dudu* in it.'

He was not perturbed. 'Bwana, would you mind pulling it out then?'

As we walked along the streets he became stickier and stickier and merely nodded his head instead of asking the usual string of questions. I tried to describe to him the tinsmith cutting and soldering pieces of kerosene tin into all manner of dishes, trays, funnels and dippers. Then I told him about the Indian shoemaker whose toes were nearly as useful as his fingers.

Coming towards us down the centre of the road were a number of Somalis dressed in bright colours with brilliant turbans. Out of their way scuttled several mangy dogs and a group of athletic chickens.

Behind us a horn blared. I grabbed Mubofu in time to swing him out of the path of a ramshackle lorry driven by an Arab. It was greatly overloaded with Africans and a varied cargo which included a depressed-looking goat.

Mubofu licked his fingers. The sugar had disappeared at an amazing rate. '*Kah*, Bwana.' His face glowed, 'I know where we are now. Is not this near the market place? Behold, I can smell the skins of cow. *Yah*, and there is the smell of things cooking and meat.'

'Your nose tells the truth. They have slaughtered a cow and all sorts of parts hang from the branches of a thorn tree. Surely it's a place of rejoicing for thousands of flies.'

He stopped, listening to Indian music blaring from worn gramophones. At last he said, '*Heh*, Bwana, it is hot.'

'Words of truth. Come and sit in the shade. Behold, in front of us now is the great *kanisa* – the cathedral.'

Mubofu sat on the top step facing away from the door which opened wide behind him. He carefully wiped his hands on the ancient rag which was his only clothing. For a time he sat listening, wrinkling his nose, trying to gain every impression that he could, then in a rather awed voice he said, 'Bwana, tell me what this great *kanisa* looks like.'

We turned and faced inside. It was very quiet and within the building our voices echoed. 'Behold, there is not a flat roof like the ordinary houses of the people but there is a dome shaped like the top of your head, and the walls are very high. Why, if six men stood one on top of each other's shoulders they could barely touch the roof.'

'*Heeh*,' breathed the boy. 'Bwana, it must reach almost to the clouds.'

'In the middle of the building, Mubofu, there are many stools, enough for six hundred people – then beyond all this is the place where they sing and preach.'

Mubofu nodded as each part was described. Three gecko lizards were walking upside-down on the domed ceiling. Their accomplishment intrigued me.

Suddenly my young friend asked, 'Bwana, can people see in heaven?'

The question caught me unprepared.

'Can they, Bwana?'

'Why, yes, Mubofu. They can, for doesn't it say in God's book, "They shall see his face"?'

'Bwana, read it to me.' He held out his hand and we walked together through the cathedral to the reading desk. There was a New Testament in Chigogo. I turned over the pages.

'Bwana, can't you feel that God is here?' His voice was hushed.

Forgetting that he could not see me, I nodded. 'Truly, Mubofu, and God is always near those of his own family. They may talk to him at any time and he talks to them by the words of his book. These are God's words about heaven. They were written by a man called John who was one of Jesus' own friends when he went about healing people who were blind and sick, before the days when evil men crucified him.

'Here is the page. These are the words, Mubofu: "They will see his face…There will be no more night. They will not need the light of a lamp or the light of the sun for the Lord God will give them light…" That's what it says about heaven.'

'Bwana, please read it again.'

I did so. He spoke in a whisper. '*Heeh*, if only I could go to heaven! But then I'm only a child and I'm blind. I can do so little.'

'Mubofu, listen. What you do doesn't matter a bit. It's what the Lord Jesus did that matters. He died so that you could go to heaven. He paid the price for your freedom.'

Mubofu nodded. 'I see, Bwana. He paid the *wulipicizo* – the freedom price.'

'Yes, it's exactly that, Mubofu. Why, in this very place years ago there were slaves but no one to buy their freedom. For us there is hope because Jesus, God's only Son, died to buy us back from a different sort of slavery.'

'Bwana, are you sure it means me too?'

'It must because Jesus said, "Whoever comes to me I will never drive away".'

'But, Bwana, what must I do? What can I say to him since I greatly want to be one of his tribe?'

'All you have to do if you want to start on the road to heaven is to ask the Lord Jesus to be your Bwana, your Lord. Then he comes into your life and with him comes everlasting life and out goes sin and its fruits. There is no place for them in the house of your life when the Son of God is there. Is he not offering you this gift of life forever? And light, not for your eyes now, but for your soul?'

The African lad stretched out both his hands in the way they do in the tribe when they receive a welcome guest. In little more than a whisper, he said, 'Almighty God, please receive me.'

The sun was well down towards the horizon. As the light streamed in through the narrow window his face lit up. I couldn't see the tragedy of his empty eyes but I could see the charm of his smile. The boy had been right when he had felt that God was there.

For a while we stood in silence and then he asked, 'Bwana, will you talk to God?'

So in his home tongue together we spoke to our heavenly Father, and then we turned and quietly walked down the passage between the three-legged stools towards the wide-open door at the back of the cathedral.

With my foot on the top step I looked down and hurriedly grabbed Mubofu by the shoulder. 'Keep absolutely still,' I ordered. 'Stay exactly where you are. Don't move your head.' Without a word he obeyed.

I reached for one of the three-legged stools, picked it up and threw it with all the force I could muster. Crash! It hit the steps. I led the small boy back into the cathedral and looked through the doorway. There, wriggling, but with its back broken, was the body of a cobra.

'What was it, Bwana?' breathed Mubofu.

'*Nzoka* – a snake – a fierce one. If you had gone one step farther, Mubofu, perhaps you would now be in heaven.'

'*Kah*,' exclaimed the boy, 'Bwana, perhaps the Lord Jesus has some work for me to do even though I'm blind.'

3

Safari and Surgery

The Indian station-master shrugged his shoulders. 'Regretfully, doctor, the news is that the train has been further delayed indefinitely. Heavy storms down the line have turned a dry gully into a roaring torrent which in turn has produced extensive washaways.'

I looked at Daudi and shook my head. 'This means trouble. Many people have come to our hospital at Kilimatinde for eye operations and we won't arrive.'

The station-master broke in. 'I hesitate to suggest, doctor, but a goods train will depart at 2100 hours going west. No comforts. You provide your own chair and lighting. I regret that the progress will be slow but you will arrive at approximately 0900 hours.'

I murmured to Daudi, '*Saa tatu* – the third hour of the morning.'

I bought our tickets. We strolled under the shade of trees. Coming towards us was Sukuma. Samson pulled up.

'Bwana, we are loaded *kabisa* - completely.'

Sukuma's springs were at full stretch. Mubofu's head was through the window. 'Bwana, my ears and my nose are telling me much.'

At that moment a locomotive whistled shrilly and puffed noisily as it shunted trucks.

'*Heeh*, I have never heard sounds like that before.'

'It is a very large machine, as big as two elephants. Inside it is a strong fire which they feed with big logs of dry wood. This boils water which makes the works inside it drive great wheels of iron...'

'Along the road that is made of iron? Have I not felt it with my feet?'

'You have found many new things today, Mubofu. That particular machine will tonight drag large trucks which contain many things. In the last one of them will be Daudi and myself. Right through the night we will move west through the thornbush and then climb along a track that winds like a snake up to the higher parts of Tanzania which lead right across to the huge lakes.'

'I'll tell him about it as we drive home,' said Samson. 'It's my country and we call it "the place where mangoes grow" – *unyaiembe*.'

'Drive back to the hospital with care, Samson. Sukuma has small joy in the bumps and potholes along the road. Behold, her back is already bent with the load she carries.'

Samson grinned as Mubofu said seriously, 'I shall speak words of caution to him, Bwana.'

'Do that,' I laughed, 'and remind him to come for us in ten days' time.'

'I will come without fail,' replied Samson.

We called, '*Kwaheri* – goodbye,' as they drove off along the Great North Road, a distinguished name for the undistinguished road that stretched from Cairo to Capetown.

I glanced at my watch. 'Nearly five hours, Daudi, before we need to return to the station. We must borrow two folding stools and a hurricane lantern for our journey.'

'We will also take food and water,' added Daudi. 'I have a friend, Daniel. His house is close. His wife cooks *ugali* with skill and *ilende* that brings joy to your palate. It is indeed a useful thing that you have learnt to eat our food our way.'

Ugali was a dry kind of porridge cooked from maize or millet flour and *ilende* was a mixture of dried herbs crushed to a powder mixed with pounded peanuts and cooked till it was jelly-like. You moulded a piece of porridge into a lump the size of a walnut, dipped it in the *ilende* which clung to it and came out looking like fine green strands of spaghetti. It required no small skill to get it from hand to mouth without tangling it.

We greeted Daniel and his wife, Marita, explained what had happened, and were at once invited to share their meal. Three-legged stools were brought and we sat watching herd boys driving hump-backed cattle home from where they had been grazing in the thornbush.

The clouds changed from pink to red to deep crimson and gold. Thousand-year-old baobab trees were silhouetted against the night sky and huge granite boulders decorating small hills looked like strawberries on a giant cream cake.

My nose stopped speaking of cattle as the *ugali* cooking in a large clay pot smelt like newly baked bread. Daniel brought a gourd of water. I held my right hand above my left hand while he poured water over them. We then prayed before starting our evening meal. With sunset came mosquitoes.

Daudi swatted one that settled on his wrist. '*Kah*! It is only since the hospital started that I realise that *mbu* – the mosquito – is the greatest danger in the land. With my microscope I find malaria in many people's blood but with quinine medicine we have strength to overcome it. One injection and POW! The *dudus* inside a man lose their strength and the fever goes.'

It always intrigued me that the best place to buy quinine was the post office. Two East African shillings – 20 cents – purchased a hundred pills. Dissolve these in distilled water and there was a powerful answer to a hundred cases of malaria.

'This medicine bites when *sindano* – the needle – goes in,' said Daniel. 'But *kumbe*, this is a thing that the people praise. A small white pill is like a pebble in the track. It is not a thing of confidence. But an injection is like a spear-thrust. It has power.'

'*Kabisa*,' agreed Daudi.

We were some five hundred kilometres south of the equator. Sunset passed quickly. In English Daudi said, 'It is now half-past six, doctor. By now Samson and Mubofu will have arrived at the hospital.'

We sat around the glowing embers talking. I listened to folk stories and joined in singing tuneful tribal songs. Daniel added rhythm with his drum.

Daudi stood up. 'I shall return very soon.' He did, carrying two folding camp stools, a hurricane lantern and a basket of paw-paws.

We thanked Daniel for our meal, lit the hurricane lamp and said, '*Kwaheri*,' as we set out for the station and our branch hospital built on the very edge of the Great Rift Wall.

We made ourselves as comfortable as we could in the steel-walled van. The whistle shrilled and with a jolt the train moved ponderously on its way along the metre-gauge track. The steel sleepers, so necessary to baffle the termites, rattled noisily. The lights of Dodoma slid behind us as the stars shone overhead. Vaguely I could see thornbush jungle on each side. Along the track behind us was a glowing trail of embers from the wood-fuelled engine. I thought of fairy tales and fiery-tailed dragons.

It was too noisy to talk and no easy matter to sit on our camp stools as the van jolted and swung from side to side. We went round a long curve and with a screaming of brakes the train pulled up at a wayside station. There was a waving of lanterns and a babble of voices as crates were unloaded.

'This is Kintinku,' said Daudi, lighting our hurricane lantern. 'Doctor, why don't we arrange these bags of millet so that we can sleep on them?'

They were not the most comfortable of beds but we managed to sleep till dawn. Early mornings are wonderful in this part of East Africa. The sunrises are a marvellous harmony of golds and reds and the air cool and stimulating.

We were climbing laboriously through a brown thornbush forest. Big hornbills screeched and flapped their wings as we approached and guinea fowl scurried off as the train went by.

'It will be a walk of eighteen kilometres,' shouted Daudi, 'from Saranda station to Kilimatinde unless Hamed, the Arab, happens to have goods on this train.'

On my last visit Hamed had had violent toothache and, as he expressed it, I had removed 'the enemy' from his jaw. He was at the station. We did get a lift.

Elephants had been active the night before along the narrow road through the thornbush. Limbs had been torn off trees and in places the undergrowth trampled flat. As we pulled up in the marketplace, people crowded round to greet us.

One grey-headed man with a large spear in his hand pushed his way to the front. 'Welcome, Bwana. Your work is greatly to be praised. See my feet. They are not scarred these days by me walking into the fire. Nor are my legs scratched from bumping into things and falling down.' He pulled down an eyelid. 'Look at my eye. I have light.'

Many people had eyes to show. Eyelids that no longer turned in. A young woman stood in my path. 'Bwana, tell me. In which eye was the ulcer that you treated on your last safari? Has it not healed *kabisa*?'

Many wanted to tell me how they had brought their relations and friends. Some had walked for two days to reach the hospital. We spent that day sorting people out and preparing for operations the next morning, working on until our own eyes protested. At the end of a week stitches were taken out and there was much rejoicing. But some whose eyes had been ruined by neglect or native medicine went home sadly. I particularly noted three who had empty eye-sockets.

They all told the same story. 'It happened, Bwana, when measles came upon us like a plague of locusts.'

The chief came to greet me. We stood on the edge of the Great Rift Wall looking out over the plains that stretched to the horizon. 'Stay longer, Bwana. There are many who need your help.' He turned and pointed with his chin to the west. 'And over there are many villages where there is no help for the sick.'

'One day, Great One, more doctors will come. But now I must return. There is the news of the coming of the disease that does so much damage to the children – *serenyenyi* - measles.'

Our return journey was without excitement – no elephants this time, just a chattering collection of monkeys and a train which arrived exactly on time, but not before I had been handed a telegram.

Tearing it open I read: *Measles epidemic spreading. Thirty deaths in nearby villages. Your return imperative.*

4

A Foretaste

The train rumbled on through the tropical night. The searchlight on the front of the engine drove a path through the thornbush jungle. In a clear patch stood three giraffes. They stood dazzled for a moment then galloped away.

The train plodded on towards Dodoma. Lights appeared ahead. For a moment I had a glimpse of

the dome of the cathedral. My mind flew to what had happened there with young Mubofu.

'*Kah*!' exclaimed Daudi. 'I can see Samson.'

The train slowed down to a crawl and pulled up at the station. It was crowded with people from a variety of tribes and nations. They were shouting to one another in a dozen languages.

Samson was pushing his way towards us. We struggled through the crowd with our luggage and medical equipment.

'*Habari* – what's the news?' I asked. In Swahili the answer is always, 'The news is good but…' and then comes the report of what actually is happening.

'The measles epidemic is here. Many children are gripped by the sickness. There is little the people can do. Truly, they need our help quickly.' We loaded up Sukuma. 'Daudi and Samson, we must work out a plan to fight measles as soon as we're back at the hospital.'

Samson cranked the car which sputtered to life, sounding like an aeroplane.

'Whatever has happened?' I asked, cupping my hands to shout.

'The exhaust pipe fell off, Bwana,' yelled Samson. 'We hope to find it on the way back.'

We drove south from the town along the rough gravel road with its familiar twists and turns. Daudi and I heard all the news of how the peanut crop was growing, about the beams in the roof of our jungle laboratory that had been attacked by white ants, and of the hospital nurse who had run away to get married.

It was three o'clock in the morning when we came to a signpost nailed to a piece of rough-cut bush timber proclaiming: To MVUMI. We turned eastward and Sukuma roared its way through dense thornbush. All of us were so tired that even the sight of eyes gleaming at us from the jungle caused no comment.

We were climbing a hill. Framed under the limbs of a great baobab tree was a mud-and-wattle house. A vague figure wrapped in a blanket waved at us from the side of the road. As we pulled up, into the head lights strode a broad-shouldered man.

'Bwana, will you come and see my son?' Then, in the local picturesque way of describing the pain of pleurisy, he added, 'He has *ihoma* – the stabbing disease.'

I pushed open the car's creaking door. 'Indeed we will come. But first we need a lantern and my bag of medicines.'

Samson was already lighting the pressure lamp and greeting the man like an old friend.

'Where are we, Daudi? And who is this man?'

"It's the village of Humbulu, doctor, and the man who greeted us is Madole, the chief and a man of much influence.'

Samson held the lamp high and we forced our way through stunted thornbush along a narrow path. We stopped at the door of the house and Madole walked through.

'*Hodi* – may I come in?' I called.

'*Karibu* – welcome, Bwana,' came a chorus of voices from the darkness.

A wave of heavy air hit me. It was thick with wood smoke and more than a hint of billy goat. In the pool of light I saw four children wrapped in blankets looking like huge cocoons. They stared at me wide-eyed.

Daudi whispered, 'Over here, doctor.'

I straightened up and bumped my head on the low roof. A handful of red mud showered down my neck and over my shoulders. Near to the mud plastered wicker-work wall, lying on a cowhide and covered by a cotton blanket, was a twelve year old. His eyes were red and swollen. Tears streamed down his face. He grunted painfully at each breath.

Daudi propped him up while I sounded his chest. There was that dull, ominous sound that meant pneumonia. The stethoscope told the same story. There was not a shadow of doubt about the diagnosis nor about the treatment he had received. Over the front of his chest were a series of deep cuts two centimetres long. Into each of these had been rubbed some native medicine. They looked angry and inflamed.

'*Kah*!' muttered Daudi, 'measles and its fierce relation, pneumonia.'

'Have you medicine that will help him?' demanded Madole.

'We have, but he needs more than just medicine. If you agree we will take him to hospital with us now, but first, *cotowa sindano* – we will give an injection.'

Madole bent his head. 'It is a thing of praise and I agree.'

Samson and Daudi linked hands and made a first-aid portable chair for the patient. Gently they carried him to the car, wrapped him in blankets and propped him up with Daudi beside him. I dissolved a tablet that would quieten his cough and reduce his pain.

I put my hands on the chief's shoulders. 'Great One, if we follow the old ways many children will die.'

He nodded. 'It is even so now. Many are ill.'

'Will you help us then? May we send trained people from the hospital to give medicine?'

He nodded. 'I agree, and will send my men to help carry it and to do your bidding.'

'Discourage those who feel that the sick ones should not sleep, those who beat drums and shake the children. If they do not sleep *ihoma* – pneumonia – stabs them and many will die.'

The boy was dozing. We called, '*Kwaheri* – goodbye' as we drove away. Ahead was a narrow riverbed, concreted, but so made that, unless you knew the road well, damage could be done both to vehicle and those in it. With a bump we were over the top. Suddenly the road seemed to disappear. We were in darkness.

'*Kah!*' Samson sounded disgusted. 'A fuse has died.'

The night seemed to close in on us. It was silent and still. I could hear the laboured breathing of the sick boy behind me. Samson lifted the front seat and was groping round in the tool box.

'*Yoh!*' he said. '*Eeeh!*'

'What's the trouble?'

'Have I not dropped the jack on my finger?'

Daudi's chuckle came through the darkness. 'I think it was in the tool box that I saw a scorpion.'

'*Hongo*,' growled Samson, 'what a pity that I have only found the fuse.'

He was vaguely silhouetted as he fumbled underneath the dashboard when, suddenly, the lights were on again. Ten places ahead of us lurked a hyaena. It slunk off out of the glare of the light.

'*Kumbe*!' Daudi's voice was full of relief. 'Is it not good to have the light again?'

As the car moved forward I said, 'If there's one thing we've learned on this safari it is the need of light. Light comes from lamps and we know that the Bible is called a lamp. Does it not tell us, "your word is a lamp for my feet and a light for my path"?'

The track swung sharply to the left. Directly ahead of us we saw a leopard with two cubs. They seemed to melt away into the tangle of thornbush. Minutes later we skidded dizzily in a patch of gravel. The headlights cut a wide swathe in the darkness and gave us a fine view of a black-maned lion walking sedately ahead of us.

'*Hongo!*' gasped Daudi. 'Everybody is out walking tonight!'

We were still estimating the size of the lion when Samson drew in his breath sharply and wrenched off a shoe. He held up a hostile-looking insect and then crushed it between his thumb and finger.

There was disgust in his voice. '*Kah*! *Dudus*.' Anything that creeps or crawls is a *dudu* in Tanzania.

I slowed to avoid a giant pothole. 'You see what I mean about light. Without it Samson would not have caught his *dudu*. Without it we would have run into hyaena and leopard and lion. But with the light not only do we see where we're going, but we are able to avoid the threatening danger of these creatures. Jesus told us, "I am the light of the world." When he has forgiven our sins and we're going his way and obeying what he says, this makes life utterly different.'

'*Eeh*,' agreed Daudi, 'and we know the way to go.' He pointed with his chin towards a pin-point of light twinkling on a hill in the distance.

We were in sight of home. The track wove in and out of a grove of baobab trees in the middle of which was a village of mud huts. In front of one of these were a group of men dancing before a campfire. The drums were beating with an odd hectic rhythm.

Daudi leaned towards me. '*Kah*, Bwana, this is a place of evil. Truly it is called Chibaya – the place of badness. Is not the chief Chikoti the most evil man in the place? Behold, he is full of pride. Does he not ride a white donkey and wear a waistcoat with silver buttons? Stealing – he thinks nothing of it. And murder to him is a small thing.'

'Isn't this the village where Mubofu lives?'

'Yes, Bwana.' He paused. 'There!' The headlights gave a glimpse of a tumbledown hut at the end of the village. 'That's where he lives and I have fears for that boy.'

There seemed to be a wall of thornbush on each side of us. '*Kah*! A place of danger, this. There are many paths leading into the swamp. There are deep holes and from here you cannot see the light on the hill.'

Daudi tapped me on the shoulder. 'Listen. We know that cough, Bwana. *Yoh*!'

'*Eheh*.' Pleurisy and pneumonia could be diagnosed without even examining the sick person. Then we all saw the twinkling light that was the hospital.

'A thing of joy,' exclaimed Samson. 'Very soon we will have this boy in bed.'

The track led through fields of millet and maize. We climbed the long hill up to the children's ward. In a matter of minutes our patient was put to bed and given treatment.

I scrambled under my mosquito net to get a couple of hours' sleep before starting to plan a counter-attack against that grim threat to childlife in Africa – a measles epidemic.

5

Plans and Demonstrations

Daudi and I stood on the verandah outside the children's ward. Madole's son had slept all night. He lay propped up in bed. My friend and assistant spoke softly, 'Already he improves. But over there...' He turned and looked out over the plains which stretched north as far as the Great Rift Wall. 'Over there in many villages children will be struck down with this evil sickness.'

'What do you think is the best way to fight it? We must work fast with carefulness or many will die and many will have ruin to their eyes. In the villages they will follow the old ways, keeping the sick ones awake. The medicine of the *waganga* – medicine men – have little value and the beating of drums to keep away hostile spirits...'

He shook his head. 'And the medicine they put into eyes...damage, damage, damage!' Daudi switched from his home language, Chigogo, to speak in careful English, 'Doctor, we must gain the confidence of the chiefs. We must show the mothers that there are medicines that have power to help.'

'If we can do that, Daudi, there are two things we must do. We need plenty of hospital space for the sick children who will come in and we must be ready to take medicines to those who won't.'

'Truly,' agreed Daudi, 'and we must be ready for mothers and grandmothers and relations who will come as well. Do not forget that many of these people have heard awful stories of what you do to patients in hospital. How you open them up with your knife while they're sleeping and take out bits of their bodies to turn into medicine and then sew them up in a way that cannot be seen. *Kumbe*, Bwana, mothers will not agree to their children staying in hospital unless they can watch everything that happens.'

I groaned. 'Must we do that, Daudi? Can't we keep them out somehow?'

'Do that and they will refuse to come and the children will suffer.'

I shook my head. 'I don't like it. It's the grandmothers I'm frightened of. They will take sick children out of bed when they have high temperatures and put them on the floor while they sleep in the beds themselves. Have we not seen it happen before?'

Daudi nodded. 'Therefore our eyes must be active to see that they do not do these things. Behold, it is better for us to have some trouble than that many children should die. Do not forget that we have Sechelela who is herself a grandmother. She has a strong tongue and knows how to deal with women, but her heart is very kind and she will tell them the words of God.'

'You're right, Daudi, that is what we will do. And I must give special training to the staff as to what measles is: how it spreads, how to deal with it and the troubles it leaves behind.'

'Truly, we must tell them what to say to the people that they may explain how the medicines work.'

'Would you please tell everybody to be here at s*aa nane* – two o'clock? After that we must get to work and make medicine by the gallon and collect all our other equipment so that tomorrow morning we may start our battle against measles in the villages.'

Daudi shook his head. 'It would be better for us to go tonight.'

'Are you sure? Wouldn't the daylight be better?'

'Go in the daytime, Bwana, and you'll find the people away scaring the birds from their crops. There'll be a few women around but they won't allow you to see the sick children. They'll push them inside the houses and tell you that all is well. But go in the night and…'

'Daudi, I don't like walking through the jungle with a hurricane lantern in one hand and a stick in the other. I dislike hyaenas intensely. Besides, I'm tired…'

Daudi spoke urgently, 'Bwana doctor, you must go. You don't yet know what measles does, but you will see tonight. And also if the children are sick with pneumonia their parents will not object to bringing them to the hospital at night because they believe there is less chance of them being bewitched if they're carried in the darkness.'

'You speak words of wisdom. We'll go tonight. Let us take Mika, the teacher with us. He is a man of understanding and will help. I'll see you and the others in the training room when the drum beats at *saa nane*.'

Exactly on time the drum started to beat with a rhythm that was strange to me. Hospital helpers streamed into the mud-brick lecture room. Old Sechelela, the senior nurse, was speaking.

'You hear that drum. You know what it says. It is the call to fight, behold, not these days with spears and knives and arrows but a deadly enemy and too small to see.'

I smiled at her. 'Grandmother, you speak words of true wisdom. That is why we're here. We need special knowledge to fight an enemy we cannot see.'

On the table in front of me I placed a small gourd containing tobacco snuff and a large, dry biscuit. I turned to one of the male nurses. 'Kefa, I want you to eat this biscuit.'

He blinked and backed away. 'Is there something wrong with it, Bwana?'

'No, it's a good biscuit but I've chosen you to eat it because you sneeze so well.'

A chuckle went round the class. The slightest whiff of tobacco snuff would start Kefa on a series of violent sneezes. True to form he crammed the biscuit into his mouth and chewed it up.

'Do you like the flavour?'

He mumbled something quite impossible to hear. His mouth was too full. I pulled the stopper from the snuff gourd, poured a little on my fingernail and flipped it in front of him. His cheeks bulged, his eyes flickered for a moment. His head moved back. He pressed violently on his upper lip but nothing could stop that sneeze.

The staff ducked. The room was showered with fine particles of dry biscuit. 'Bwana,' gasped Kefa, 'I'm sorry, I...' He sneezed again. 'I can't help...' Again he sneezed. 'It's your fault. It's the...' Again an explosion interrupted his sentence.

'Thank you, Kefa,' I replied. 'You've done all I wanted and done it splendidly.' I turned round to the staff. 'You have seen?'

'*Kah*!' snorted Daudi. 'Why did you do it, Bwana? It's an evil thing to sneeze food all over a room and all over people.'

Samson snorted with disgust. '*Yoh*! I have no joy in this thing.'

'You weren't meant to. I meant to upset you, to show you in a way that you'll find hard to forget that sneezing and coughing are a common way of making people ill, of spreading disease. You can see bits of biscuit but you cannot see the tiny germs and their vicious relations, the viruses, which a sneeze sprays in thousands and thousands over everybody within five metres.'

Kefa blew his nose. '*Koh*, I did not know that.'

'Maybe, but you'll never forget it now. And a cough is just as dangerous unless you cover up your mouth.'

'*Heeh*,' protested Kefa, 'if I had covered my mouth crumbs would have come from my ears.'

Samson grinned. 'This is a thing of laughter: his mouth too full of biscuit, his eyes sticking out, and a sneeze arriving which he could not stop.' Everyone laughed.

'I was not trying to amuse you but to warn you of danger. I'm sharing with you plans to fight this epidemic that threatens our country. Measles is not a germ. It is much smaller even than that. It is a virus. No ordinary microscope will show it. One child has it in his throat. His nose streams, his eyes run, he sneezes and coughs, spraying the danger. Behold, other children catch the trouble. Therefore let us teach people to put sick children in a separate part of the house, or, better still, to bring them here to hospital so that measles may not spread through the whole of the family, through the whole of the village, like a fire through a dry cornfield.'

I produced a second box and took from it a bottle of yellow medicine, a small bottle of black eye drops and a vinegar bottle labelled with a death's head and POISON written underneath it in three languages. 'These are our spears and bows and arrows, our rifles and guns to use in this battle. The yellow mixture is for coughs: to soothe them, to bring down the temperature. The eye drops: put them into the children's eyes and they will take away the redness and the swelling and save many an eye from blindness. And the medicine in the long bottle is special. It is two things: a liniment to rub on chests because in it is stuff called menthol that cools the skin; at the same time the smell of it finds its way up the child's nose and helps them to breathe better.'

There was a general nodding of heads. 'Yes, Bwana, we understand.'

'There will be four teams, each of three people. The leader will write the name of the sick one in the book and also the pulse and the number of times the child breathes each minute – we call it the respiration rate. Kefa, how many times do you breathe each minute?'

Kefa concentrated. 'About sixty, Bwana.'

I smiled across at Daudi. 'What do you think of that?'

'That's the rate of a dog who has run very far without a drink. '

'You're right. Now, everybody, please count your own breathing,' I ordered, glancing at my watch. 'Start now.'

There was a considerable nodding of heads and when I said 'Stop' the results varied from fourteen to twenty. 'Now, you leaders, if anyone breathes more than thirty times a minute put a red cross after that name in your book. Write down how much medicine you give, whether you use eye drops and if you rub their chests, and of course their pulse, their temperature and their respiration.'

Daudi rolled his eyes. '*Koh*, Bwana, it is much work.'

'But work that will save lives. As well as the leader there is a nurse who gives the drinking medicine. She carries a big bottle of medicine on her head. The third member of the team treats eyes and chests. First he cleans the eyes and puts in drops. Afterwards he rubs chests and…' I turned questioningly to the class.

'Washes his hands, Bwana.'

I nodded. 'And, Daudi, all leaders must see that sick children are kept inside in a clean part of the house away from other children. They must have plenty of water to drink and make sure that none of the relations beats drums, shouts, or does anything else to keep them awake.'

'We will do this,' agreed Daudi, 'but it will not be easy. We will do all these things and will tell them the words of health. They will see that we can save life and save eyes and bring joy to sad hearts.'

'One thing more,' I added, 'before you go. Remember, we do not only make people better who are sick. We are not fighting just the sickness of people's bodies. It may well be that there is the opportunity to tell people of a worse disease than measles, the one that kills every time, not bodies but souls.'

'*Yoh*,' said Sechelela, 'I read it this morning in the book that John wrote. "You did not choose me but I chose you to go and bear fruit, fruit that will last." Are we not like trees, Bwana?'

'You are, Seche, but what profit is there in a mango tree if there are only leaves on it?'

'*Koh*,' interrupted Kefa, 'you can't eat leaves.'

'True. And what is the value of a banana palm?'

 Samson was on his feet. 'You can use the bark for wrapping parcels, Bwana, and the leaves as a sort of umbrella but, *heeh*, it's the fruit that brings joy to your stomach.'

'Your words have strength, Samson. It's fruit that matters. God expects all of us to use our opportunities not only to help the people who have measles but to show by what we do and how we do it that we belong to God.'

6

Reconnaissance

'Here are the thermometers and the exercise books, Daudi. Also the bottles of medicine for coughs and the drops for the eyes.'

My assistant held up a miniature version of an hourglass. 'I like these things, doctor. They measure a half minute better than most watches, and certainly better than the old alarm clock that Kefa likes so much.'

I smiled. 'Daudi, let's go over the general plan of our campaign.' Daudi nodded. 'My team and I will go to a village and speak to the chief. If he and his people are willing to accept our help I shall write the names of the sick children in the book and order the medicines and treat the eyes. Mboga will count pulses and respiration rates and take temperatures and then will rub chests with liniment. Mwendwa will give the medicines and explain to the women about looking after the sick ones. We may have to change things a bit after we have worked for a day or two.'

'Good. I think that is the general plan as things stand at the moment.'

All at once it seemed to grow dark in the dispensary. Through the mosquito gauze of the window we saw a great black cloud sweeping across the sky. There was a distant rumble of thunder. The storm was coming our way. There was a jagged flash of lightning followed almost at once by a crash of thunder. Then the rain came. It pelted down.

The hills that half an hour before had stood out green against the blue of the sky were curtained by the downpour. There was a frenzied shifting of beds in the hospital to avoid the leaks that came through the roof. People dashed out into the downpour putting dishes, basins, tubs – anything that would hold water – under the cascades that came from the roof. A few minutes' work now could save tedious journeys to the wells two kilometres away.

Mboga, a cheerful male nurse with a robust sense of humour, put his head round the door. '*Yoh*, Bwana. Is it not music to hear the water running into the tanks?

This will bring joy to those who dig in their gardens and the millet and the maize will grow with strength.' He disappeared as suddenly as he had arrived.

'*Hongo*,' said Daudi, 'those are words of truth, but when we go tonight it will be on foot through six kilometres of black mud and six more of them on the way back. *Kah*!'

The disgust that he put into this last typically African expression was more than warranted.

We set out that evening, Daudi leading. I came second and behind me Mika. As we walked carefully down the slippery banks of a riverbed the old man said, 'Bwana, in the days when this country was German East Africa, in the village where our hospital is now, more than half the children died in a month from measles. The medicines of the tribe did nothing and the medicines they used then are the same as they use now.'

'*Eheh*,' agreed Daudi, 'and many years later when I was a small boy it happened again. My elder brother and sister both died but I got better. I was only three but I can still remember the beatings of tins and drums all through the village. There was constant noise, with people screaming, some of them to keep the children awake, some because their children would wake no more. I can still feel the beat of those drums and the clashing of those tins throbbing in my head.'

He stopped and raised a finger. 'Listen to them now.'

Far out beyond a grove of baobab trees came a faint sound. It meant little to me but to Daudi it woke memories that he would never be able to erase. He spoke through clenched teeth, 'I am going to avenge my brother and sister, avenge them a hundred times in this epidemic.'

'In what way, Daudi?'

'Bwana, I am going to walk till my feet will walk no further. I am going to talk to the village people till my tongue swells and, with God's help, we'll save many lives. I'll...'

The old teacher interrupted. 'Be careful, Daudi. You're young. You have learnt much but don't forget that the people listen to the words of the witchdoctor and the medicine man and believe them rather than the words of the doctor. It is the custom of the tribe.'

'Truly,' agreed Daudi, 'but we must use all the wisdom that we have.'

The old man nodded. 'But do not forget that it says in God's book, "If any man lacks wisdom let him ask of God".'

'You're right, Mika,' I answered. 'We can't deal with this problem by ourselves. We know ways to help noses that run and eyes that are inflamed and to stop coughs from turning to pneumonia, but we need the help of God when we meet those who refuse to listen or have hostility in their words.'

'Agreed,' said Mika. 'We must have strength in what we say but not anger. Should we not ask God for wisdom?' He hesitated, 'And for protection?'

We all knew that within a few hours' walk of where we stood were thousands of children.

In the warm darkness of the tropical night we asked Almighty God that our efforts to deal with this scourge would have success. For some ten minutes we plodded on, each engrossed in his own thoughts. Daudi, who was walking in front carrying a hurricane lantern, picked his way through a tangle of stunted thornbush. Thick black mud squelched ankle-deep beneath our feet and I could feel it finding its way through the lace-holes of my shoes and oozing clammily between my toes.

Suddenly the light ahead of me disappeared. There was a crash and a gasp. I stopped and switched on an electric torch and there below me sat Daudi beside the ruins of the hurricane lantern. The storm had created a flash flood and had torn a soil erosion channel three metres wide and a metre deep through this low-lying piece of country. Daudi had stepped uncomfortably into space. He sat there looking at me owlishly, still clinging to the handle of the lamp.

Mika's voice came behind me. '*Yoh!* He has fallen.'

Daudi looked up at me ruefully. 'Bwana, I was thinking deep thoughts and looking at the stars and, *koh*, I fell all right! Behold, our lamp is no more.' He struggled to his feet covered with sticky black mud that had an odd musty smell about it.

'*Yoh*,' grinned Daudi. 'It is clear that this is a place greatly favoured by many cattle.'

We pulled him out and with care walked on in the starlight for half a kilometre. Flickering ahead of us was a camp fire. Men sat silently round it, their shadows twisted and distorted on the wall of the mud-and-wattle house behind them. I felt icy shivers going up my spine for from inside that house came a sickening din, the thumping of tins and the beating of drums with the sole purpose of preventing sleep.

As we came into the firelight the men started to their feet. Mika spoke for us. 'Good evening to you,' he said in Chigogo.

'And good evening to you,' they replied.

'We come to you,' said the old teacher, 'to help the children who are sick. With us is the doctor. He has medicines.'

A woman suddenly rushed past us, screaming, her scream ending in a shrill, high-pitched, hysterical note. She ran blindly into the darkness.

'What happened to her, Daudi?' I asked in a whisper.

He turned to one of the men, mumbled a few words and then explained, 'Bwana, three of her children have died in two days.'

The chief had risen to his feet. 'If you can help our children we will receive your medicine.'

Daudi whispered, 'He opens the door to us. Let us go round the village.'

Each flat-roofed mud-and-wattle house held its own tragedy.

An old woman crouched moaning in a dark corner. I bent down beside her. 'What's wrong, grandmother?'

'*Heehee*,' she muttered. 'My grandchildren are no more – all of them, all of them.'

In the background I could see vague shadows moving. 'What are they doing, Daudi?'

'They do not bury the children, Bwana. They take them out into the thornbush and leave them.'

The eerie howl of a hyaena answered my unasked question and then I saw my first measles case which had been treated by the medicine man. In the smoky atmosphere of the house six children lay huddled together on a grass mat, their eyes matted with discharge, their noses streaming and one of them breathing at a rate which showed clearly that he was on the verge of pneumonia. Beside them were three other little folk including the baby. As far as I could see they had not yet been infected.

'Come, Daudi. Let's go to work.'

We did what we could for them. They were given cough mixture loaded with a sedative so strong that they would sleep despite the noise. Daudi touched my shoulder. 'Let's go outside and pretend to go away and watch what happens.'

Minutes later we peered through a crack in the mud wall. Already two of the children had fallen asleep, the sleep of exhaustion. But an old woman had come out of the shadows and was shaking one child. He woke with a start. She could not rouse the second child so she poured cold water over him and dragged him out into the night wind.

Daudi exploded into words so forceful that the old woman gasped and shuffled off into the darkness. The children were soon made comfortable and put to sleep again.

Mika arrived with the chief and we gave our instructions, promising next day that a team would arrive to treat the children. 'Great One,' I urged, 'it is a matter of high importance that the children should sleep.'

He nodded and Mika explained, 'I have spoken with many words. They are understood and they will be obeyed.'

Our visit to the various houses brought to light seven children in the early stages of pneumonia who would be taken to hospital first thing the next morning.

As I farewelled the chief said, 'We have seen your medicine and the way you use it. It is a matter for praise. But at Chibaya, the next village, they will have nothing to do with you or your medicines.'

Mika had borrowed a hurricane lantern. He urged me. 'Bwana, we should return to the hospital now. There is small wisdom in going to that next village into hostility. They're bad men there.'

I shook my head. 'Come on. We're spying out the land. We mustn't stop now. Let's go to the worst place of all and see what Chibaya is really like.'

7
Blind Boy to the Rescue

By the light of our borrowed lantern we walked on towards the hostile village. The path was rough, gashed here and there with deep muddy creeks. In one creek a hyaena stood looking at us, snarled and then slunk away.

Mika shook his head. 'It is not too late to turn back. We're walking into trouble. Let us return. The night is late already and we have but one lantern.' But I was impelled to push on. We could see the fires of Chibaya and hear the beat of the drums.

'*Koh*,' said Daudi, 'that is not a good dance, Bwana.'

On the night wind came the reek of native beer. From the far end of the village a high scream of a woman was almost drowned by the hectic throb of drums.

'It's an evil place,' muttered Daudi.

Walking into the firelight I greeted the chief, who was dressed in a long, flowing garment called a *kanzu*.

Over it he wore his famous waistcoat decorated with silver buttons. He was sufficiently drunk to be aggressive, as were his men. Several of them picked up spears and sticks and moved closer to us.

'Bwana Chikoti,' I said quietly. 'We have come to offer help if there are any children in your village suffering from serenyenyi.'

'There are no sick people in my village,' he growled in a thick voice. 'And also, we do not want your medicine.'

'Is there any profit in losing the lives of the children of your village?'

'*Kah*!' he shouted. 'We do not want the medicine of the *wazungu* – the Europeans. Have we not our own *waganga* – witchdoctors?'

'But what of your women-folk? What of their sorrow in seeing their children die? Do they suffer for nothing?'

'*Koh*!' roared Chikoti. 'Is this village run by women?' He staggered towards me brandishing a knobbed stick.

Daudi seized my arm. 'Let's go. When there is much *wujimbi* – beer – there is little wisdom. This *shauri* – discussion – will only lead to big trouble.'

As I nodded I turned to Chikoti. 'Remember we have powerful medicine for coughs and can draw the teeth of the strongest pain.'

'*Heh*!' jeered one of his young men. 'We do not want the herbs you cook.' He staggered forward and crashed his *knobkerrie* - knobbed stick - into the lamp I carried. There was a roar of scornful laughter.

'Bwana,' urged Mika, 'come. They're only waiting for an excuse to make bad trouble.'

A huge clay pot of beer had just been brought. The dancers crowded round it drinking and shouting noisily. Drums throbbed an ominous rhythm. Hastily we retreated out of the firelight followed by high-pitched jeering laughter. We hurried off into the darkness. The batteries of my torch were nearly flat but we were able to gauge our direction by the Southern Cross which was low down on the horizon.

There was a rumble of thunder. Clouds rolled over the sky and the stars seemed to go out. An intense darkness swallowed us up as sudden flashes of lightning warned us of the dangers of the path. There were gaping holes ahead and thornbush seemed to close in around us. It was as though all manner of strange and dangerous shapes lurked there. From behind us at Chikoti's village came wild, scornful shouting.

Mika's voice came out of the darkness beside me. 'They are not just laughing at us but at God. Do they not follow the ways of *shaitan* – the devil?'

For a time we walked on, the track becoming rougher and rougher. A branch of thornbush slashed across my face. 'Ohhh!' I gasped. 'I don't like this.'

'We're off the path,' said Daudi. 'We're lost and in front of us is hooked thornbush and the swamp called Chipoko.'

There were a few matches left in the box. I struck one but the high wind quickly blew it out. Just beyond us a hyaena howled. I felt my skin creep. Again thunder crashed and, following it, dead silence.

In that silence came a voice, 'Bwana! Bwana!'

'Who is it? Who calls?'

'It is I, Mubofu.'

'Where are you?'

Daudi put out his hand. 'Bwana, hold my arm and we will walk together towards the voice.'

In a moment we came to where the blind boy was standing in the middle of the path. 'I heard all that happened,' he said, 'and I crept away from my house.

Behold, when you live as I do in the land of darkness, day and night are the same and the path to the hospital is known to me whether the sun shines or not. Behold, now in the darkness you know for a short time how I always feel. But, Bwana, it is here that I am useful. Many times people have led me by the hand, but it is tonight that I will lead you.'

I put my hand into his, and with Daudi and Mika linking up we set out on the six kilometre walk back to the hospital on the hill.

8
Scars

Mubofu stepped out confidently. The darkness was intense, visibility nil. I shielded my eyes as rain beat into our faces but the blind boy never hesitated. From time to time he would warn of a tree or a gap in the path. He was excited.

'Tonight it is splendid to be blind, to have feet that know the path, every footstep of it.' He laughed. 'Truly, this is a wonderful night for me.' Then, abruptly, 'Walk carefully. There is a giant baobab tree near here and its roots grow far out. We are coming to it now. Soon we must move a little to the north for there is a large stone, big as a lorry. Here it is. Feel it.' I did so. 'Hear how the water rushes down from the hills!'

We had to wade through three torrents of muddy water

69

cascading from the hills. In the last of these I slipped and was not only bedraggled but very muddy. Pausing to get my breath, Daudi suddenly exclaimed, 'See, a light!'

'It must be the hospital,' said Mika. 'Where else would there be lights at this time of the night?'

Beside me I felt Mubofu stiffen. 'If you can see now, Bwana, there is no need for me to lead any more.'

'You're still greatly needed, Mubofu. The light is only like a small star.'

We started again and the light gradually became larger as Mubofu unhesitatingly led up the track warning us sharply of some rut or twist or stone. The light on the hill proved to be not in the hospital but in the window of my own house. I found the kitchen door open and on the stove a kettle was boiling merrily. Mubofu was shivering. He moved as close as he could to the fire. Water dripped from his tattered loincloth. I made tea and poured out a cup for each of my companions. The warmth of the drink was most welcome.

I put a slice of bread and honey into the boy's hand. 'It would be wise for you stay at the hospital tonight. You're cold. We'll give you a blanket and a mat and you may sleep in the room where Daudi makes medicines.'

Mubofu shook his head vigorously. '*Ngo, ngo* – no, no, Bwana. I must get back to the village. I have work to do. Is not this my task to bring the children who are sick to the hospital? Must I not do my work by night?'

'But you're cold and it's a bad night for anyone to

be out. Better to rest quietly here today...'

The African boy interrupted me. 'No, Bwana, I must do this work. No one else in Chibaya cares for God. Did you not see them tonight? Behold, will they not be very drunk before long and then, while their wisdom is sleeping, perhaps I can find those who need help and who could come quietly in the darkness. Behold, I'll get them to the hospital and you will be able to

help them here.'

'*Lunji* – perhaps – but we met Chikoti face-to-face and he is a fierce man. If you do these things secretly will he not have heavy anger and come to the hospital with much noise?'

Daudi shook his head. 'No, Bwana, I don't think he'll make much noise but he will make much trouble. He's a *fundi* – an expert – in all sorts of evil ways.'

The blind boy put his hand on my shoulder. 'Are you afraid of trouble when it means the children will be saved from much sickness and you will have the chance of telling the people of my village about God?'

'No, Mubofu, I'm not frightened of trouble nor its consequences to myself, but what about you?'

'*Kah*, Bwana. Must I only show my thanks to Jesus in a safe way? If there is pain in the work that lies ahead, was there no pain when they killed my Saviour?'

There was silence in the kitchen. Moths beat their wings against the glass of the hurricane lantern and on the corrugated iron roof great drops of rain from the baobab tree beside the house splashed noisily.

Mubofu was the first to speak. 'Bwana, a moment ago when my hand was on your arm I felt scars.'

I looked down and saw the vaccination marks on my arm. 'Yes, those show me that I need have no fear of the smallpox disease, which is very much worse than measles can ever be.'

'*Hongo*, Bwana,' said the African boy. 'How can you be sure of that?'

'Hundreds and thousands of people have been treated in this way. It has been proved by what has happened to them. They have lived in places where there is much of this disease and it has not attacked them.'

Mubofu shook his head. 'But, Bwana, this is a thing of wonder. Tell me, how does it work?'

There, sitting in front of the fire, I told him the story of Dr Jenner and how he had discovered the value of vaccination. The blind boy was all interest and wanted to know details.

'But, Bwana, how… how does it work? How is it done?'

'A calf is given the sickness called cow pox by injection with a needle. Then they wait for some days before they collect from the calf what is called lymph. Your arm is then scratched with a needle and a drop of this lymph put into the scratch. Behold, you get a little of the trouble, some pimples on your arm, and you are then free from the danger of the smallpox disease.'

'*Kumbe*, Bwana,' said Mubofu, 'but what happens to the calf?'

'Oh, the calf is looked after with care. They see that it does not suffer.'

'But, mightn't the calf die of the disease?'

'Yes, it might, but it's not at all likely.'

'Bwana, if it did die would it not be happy if it could know that it had saved people from a deadly disease?'

Daudi broke into the conversation. 'Mubofu, do you not understand that that is exactly what Jesus did? Calves cannot understand, but Jesus knew before he came into the world that he would die to rescue us from the worst disease that there is – the disease of sin which shuts us out from eternal life.'

Mubofu sat with his head in his hands and his words were firm. 'It is because I understand that I am going back to my village tonight.'

His finger moved quietly up my arm. 'Bwana, I wish I had scars on my arm like yours. It would give me comfort and I would not feel the danger of the smallpox disease.'

I poured out another cup of tea. 'Listen and I will tell you the story of a man who lived when Jesus was on earth. He said that unless he could touch the scars in Jesus' hands and the spear wound in his side he would not believe that Jesus had come to life again.'

'*Kah*, Bwana,' said Mubofu, 'but Jesus died and he was buried. Did he not die? He is not alive!'

'But he is,' I replied. 'That is why our faith in Jesus is a certain faith. Do not many follow a prophet called Mohammed? He was a man and he died. But Jesus claimed to be God's own Son. While he was alive on earth he said that he would rise from the dead three days after he was buried. And he did. Was he not seen by hundreds of people?'

'*Kah!*' exclaimed Mubofu. 'That is a thing of wonder. He is alive?'

'Truly, we work for a living master, not a dead memory. Let me finish telling you about the man called Thomas who did not believe even when he heard the words of those who had seen Jesus alive. He said, "Unless I can put my finger in the scars of his hands and the scar in his side I will not believe".

'One night many of Jesus' followers were all together in one room. Thomas, the doubter, was there. The doors were all shut but suddenly Jesus was amongst them. He greeted them and he turned at once to Thomas and said, "Feel the scars in my hands, the scars in my feet, the scar in my side". In a second Thomas's doubts disappeared and he said, "My Lord and my God".'

Mubofu stood in silence. 'Then I saw his hand move slowly to his face and touch his scarred eyes, scarred through disease and the dangerous futility of native medicine and treatment. Daudi put his hand on the boy's shoulder.

'There is no shame in a scar. It may be that your scar will prove to be the way of healing to those who are sick and even at this minute are groaning.'

Mubofu reached for the stick that was beside him and said as he picked it up, 'Bwana, I must return to my village. Behold, there is work for me to do.'

'Before you go let us all talk to our living Lord and tell him of our work and our difficulties.'

We prayed together, then I watched the blind boy walk off into the darkness. After only a few steps he was lost in the blackness of the night. As we stood at the door watching, suddenly the whole place was lit by a flash of lightning. Well on his way in the centre of the track it showed us Mubofu, walking confidently towards one of the most sinister villages in all Tanzania.

9
Chibaya

Daudi and I stayed at the kitchen door hoping to catch a last silhouette of the blind boy's figure as he walked through the millet gardens and the thornbush, but he was completely swallowed up in the darkness.

'Bwana, it is a good thing in many ways that this night is wet. Behold, there are not many animals about on a night like this and his journey is safer that way. Also, there are no snakes. *Kumbe*! They must be his biggest danger for he cannot see them and often they will move right out into the path at night because it is warmer there.'

I listened to the welcome musical sound of water running into our large storage tank.

'Daudi, apart from Mubofu, is there anybody at Chibaya who is likely to help us, even though his help may be only small?'

My assistant thought for a moment. 'Yes, Bwana, there is a man who will help. His name is Ndogowe

– the donkey. Behold, was he not the man who looked after Chikoti's white donkey? He got into bad trouble and was saved from it by the skill of Bibi Dobson, who was a nurse here before you came. But, Bwana, that is a long story. I will tell it to you as we go on safari one day.'

'Right. I have need of sleep now. There is much work ahead of us.'

Daudi splashed off towards his home at the hospital after bidding me 'Kwaheri – goodbye'.

Soon, thankfully, I was in bed. The rain had ceased but the wind was blowing strongly and the shutters, made from box wood, were rattling noisily. As I dozed off, this sound became mixed with the wailing of a broken-hearted mother that I had heard at Chibaya earlier in the evening. I seemed to have slept for only a few minutes when a voice outside the fly-wire of my window wakened me. 'Bwana, hodi – may I come in, Bwana?'

'What's the matter?' I asked.

'Bwana…' there was urgency in the tone. 'It is I, Mubofu. I am here with many sick ones.'

I glanced at my watch. It was five o'clock in the morning. Turning my torch to the window, I saw Mubofu with a child of about seven years of age on his back. The boy looked so desperately ill that I wondered for a moment if he were still alive. I could vaguely see three or four other people standing against the white-washed wall of the house. I pulled on some clothes and my mosquito boots and hurried outside.

'Come, let us go at once to the hospital.'

All traces of the storm a few hours before had disappeared. Eerily through the standing corn came the laugh of a hyaena. I took them into our outpatients' room. The night nurse had seen us coming. She lifted the child from Mubofu's back. The blind boy sank down, exhausted, on the floor. I wrapped the boy in a blanket and laid him on a bed. He had advanced measles. His skin seemed to burn. He was breathing thirty-two times to the minute. Listening with a stethoscope to his chest made it clear that he had pneumonia. He was one of the many who would develop pneumonia if this epidemic was left to itself.

Mubofu sat up, the blanket wrapped round him. 'Who is he, Mubofu?'

'His name is Mazengo, Bwana, and he is the grandson of chief Chikoti. 'He comes with me secretly to hear the words of God on Sunday.'

'This could make things interesting,' I murmured, lighting a spirit lamp and preparing an injection for the sick boy.

Mubofu moved close to me. 'Bwana, what are you doing?'

I explained, 'In this instrument, which has a hollow sharp needle on the end of it, I have medicine which brings sleep and quietness. Behold, Mazengo is exhausted after his journey.'

'*Eheh*, Bwana, I too am tired. Have I not carried him all the way on my back?'

'Sit there Mubofu, and keep warm. Before long I shall give you food.'

'*Heeh*, Bwana.' There was a smile round his lips.

'That splendid food which was sweet?'

I put my arm round him. 'That is the food that you will eat.'

Mubofu sank down wearily on a box.

I gave Mazengo the injection and saw him being carried to the ward in Mwendwa's arms.

Perisi, the night nurse, came to me. 'Bwana, there are two women here with small children. Both of them have measles. Both are very sick. Behold, each of these women tells me that two of their children have already died and they have come to the hospital for help. They see no hope in the medicines of the *waganga*.'

'Make beds for them in the small room that we use to store the soap and the blankets. There is just room there. Give them the cough medicine and put drops in their eyes. I will come soon.'

Mubofu gripped my arm. 'Bwana, I must leave the hospital before it is light. I do not want the people of my village to know who brought Mazengo here. If they did, things might happen and I might not be able to help others.'

It was clear that he was right. From a cupboard I took bread, cut two thick chunks and spread them liberally with honey. I put them into his hand. 'Go home and sleep in the day time and eat this on the way.'

He stretched out both hands to take it from me. '*Asante*, Bwana.'

Again I put my arm around him. 'Mubofu, let me give you not only food for your body but a message from God's book which you may think of today and in the days that are to come as we fight for people's bodies and their souls. Once there was a man called Joshua. God chose him to do special work. And the words he said to Joshua, Mubofu, he says to you, "I will be with you. I will not fail you or forsake you. Be strong and of good courage".'

He held onto my hand. 'Bwana, these are great words. Behold, since you told me that Jesus is a living Saviour I have had great joy in my heart. And now you tell me that he will be with me. Truly, I will do everything I can to work for him.'

'This is a thing of merit. But you must sleep if you are to carry this work through. You must have strength to make these secret safaris.'

He nodded agreement. 'I know it must be done secretly, for chief Chikoti will stop people from coming to hospital if he finds out how they are getting here.'

Halfway through a busy morning Daudi came to see me. 'Bwana, I have found the man, Ndogowe, who was bitten by the donkey. He says we have no fear of trouble from Chibaya for at least two days for the chief and the other elders of the village have been drinking much beer and also *nghangala* – native mead.' This I knew to be the most intoxicating drink, made from bush honey, which would keep even so experienced a drinker as Chikoti out of circulation for some time.

I grinned. 'The news is good. Daudi, tell me about this fellow, Ndogowe.'

Daudi chuckled. 'What a story it is. You know the donkey that Chikoti rides, the white one? It is a valuable ass and therefore badly spoiled and most stubborn. Does not the chief have it fed on porridge like a child? One day Ndogowe brought the animal's food in a dish but the donkey was in a bad temper and snapped at him and bit off the end of his nose.' Daudi put his thumb in his fingers to show how much nose the bite had removed!

'*Heeh*, Daudi, what then?'

'Bwana, it's hard to believe. He picked up his nose,

or rather, the bit that was bitten off, jumped onto a bicycle and rode hard to the hospital. *Yah*, Bwana, what a mess. *Heeh*! It makes my insides creep even now. But those of the hospital were not upset. The sister bathed his nose, boiled up a needle and some horse-hair and sewed it on again. Then she put a dressing on it and kept everything in place with cotton wool and sticking plaster.'

'*Hongo*, Daudi, but what happened? Did it heal well?'

'Yes, Bwana, that was the amazing thing. It healed without any trouble whatsoever. The only thing that worried him was the tip to his nose wasn't in the same place as it was before the donkey bit him.'

'Was he happy about it all?'

'*Eeh*, Bwana, was he happy! Why, he talked and talked and brought us pawpaws and sweet potatoes. Then at Christmas time he brought a young goat which we killed and cooked and Bibi said she had never tasted a lamb like it!'

With laughter I continued, 'But tell me, Daudi. What help are we going to get from this man?'

'All we can hope for is that he will tell us what is happening in the village. He will not do anything, but he will be eyes and ears for us in a place where we have few to help.'

'What an odd team we've got in Chibaya to fight against this epidemic, Daudi – a blind boy and a man whose nose was bitten off by a donkey!'

10
Reports

I sat with four sheets of paper in front of me. The heat was intense. Through the window I could see the plain with a beautiful stretch of blue water in the middle of it. Its colourful coolness was most attractive but I knew that where the lake appeared to be there was nothing but dry land, scarred soil erosion, where nothing would grow. It was a mirage.

Daudi came in. 'What do you see over there, Daudi?'

He laughed. 'I see much water which one cannot drink.' He sank down wearily on a stool opposite me. '*Yah*, and it's like many of the difficult people I have been trying to help in this battle against measles.'

He picked up one of the reports. With a wry smile he said, 'You see I took all the difficult places. The easy ones where they wanted our help I sent Kefa, and with him went Hilda. Kefa is a mild man but Hilda, although small, *h-e-e-e-h* she's got a tongue and behold she can...she can.. what are the English words, Bwana?'

'Tick off?'

'Yes,' Daudi nodded. 'She can tick off people who are difficult and will not obey. *Yoh*, how she can tick them off!'

Laughing, I read at the bottom of Kefa's report, '107 children treated in three villages, three families difficult, dealt with by Hilda while I went next door and took temperatures.' Daudi's smile was wide as I read this to him.

'I would like to have been there, Bwana.'

I raised my eyebrows. 'You are not bad at ticking people off yourself!'

'Maybe, but I tick them with care, with great gentleness. You see, there was the chief at Makanga. He refused to allow me to take medicine to the children of his town and then he asked me for pills to deal with his headache, so I told him that headaches could be caused by many things. They were often due to mosquito bites, which give malaria, and I told him of the chief who had died from severe malaria. It brought him no joy to hear this.'

I sat back in my chair. 'And then, I suppose, Daudi, you told him about meningitis and sun-stroke?'

'Yes, Bwana, I did – and eye troubles and the bad sorts that send you blind. In fact I told him of every disease that I could think of and when he was thoroughly worried I told him there were no pills for him unless the measles children were treated as well.

86

He agreed, so I promised medicine after the children had been treated. There were sixty-three sick children in that village alone. Forty or more had already died. There will be a big change there now.' He yawned. 'Since before dawn we have been at it, telling them to sweep out their houses...the filth, the cockroaches, *ugh*!'

He wrinkled his nose humorously.

'But I have the children's treatment going well, putting in eye drops, pouring out much medicine. *Yoh*, my arms ache! I have counted pulses and breathing and watched chests being rubbed. I have walked away from the village and then come back running to make sure they were not following the ways of the witchdoctor.' He produced a notebook. 'Seventeen new children are coming to hospital. With them is the risk of pneumonia. And, *yoh*, Bwana.' Again he stretched and yawned.

'Are you tired, Daudi?'

'Not so much tired, Bwana. I don't yawn when I'm tired but I do when I'm hungry.'

Samson's smiling face appeared in the doorway. 'Behold, you must have a famine inside you if you are like me, Bwana. Daudi gave me what he thought would be the hardest villages.'

Daudi shook his head. 'I did not. I kept them for myself.'

'Well,' growled Samson, 'if mine were easy ones, your work must have been difficult indeed. Bwana, there was a chief who refused help. He wouldn't even let me into his village. He, by the way, is a friend of Chikoti. He forbade people to follow our way. He said that they would die if anyone did and I began to despair. But silently, with my eyes open, I prayed to God and asked him to help and it was then that an old man came out of a house. He was a visitor. He walked over to me and greeted me and said to the chief, "They have medicines that work at that hospital and the Bwana there, although he is a white man, can do things which we are unable to do with our witchdoctor's medicine. Behold, was I not blind? Did I not pay out cows and goats to the *waganga* and yet nothing happened? *Kah!*" He spoke with disgust, "I tried many medicines, many charms, but still darkness. But the Bwana worked with his little knife and I can see…"'

'Who was he, Samson?'

'*Heeh*,' chuckled Samson, 'that's the joke. He's the old man who refused to pay his "thank you" when you did his cataract operation because he said he was no better. He stormed at you. He said that the hospital was no good and that the witchdoctor had the best of medicines.'

Daudi laughed at the memory. 'He said things that the Bwana could not understand but which you and I did! I remember feeling hot under my skin.'

'Do you remember,' Samson went on, 'that instead of using angry words the Bwana said to him that he would ask God that his eyes might get completely better. Then he told us of the words of King Solomon that "a soft answer turns away wrath".'

'I remember,' agreed Daudi, 'and I thought he was wrong.'

'He wasn't,' declared Samson, 'for this old man had

nothing but good to say about our work and, behold, because of his words I treated thirty children in that village. The chief came with me and when one man refused medicine the chief threatened to fine him. Drops were put into the children's eyes and those who beat kerosene tins were silenced. And, Bwana, I have a new way of helping to keep the children quiet.'

'And what's that, Samson?'

He grinned. 'Behold, many people come asking for medicine for headaches, for pains in their joints, and I give them not only the aspirin pills but the bromide pills as well. Behold, they are tired already. When they take the bromide pills they sleep for many hours.'

Daudi laughed. 'Bwana, that's an old trick.'

'Maybe,' agreed Samson, 'but it's a good trick.'

I collected their reports. My measles flying squad in one day had treated five hundred children. They had found twelve cases of pneumonia and two of severe eye trouble. These little folk were already in hospital. It was only a matter of time and they would be well. I picked up a pencil and was writing out orders for the next day when Kefa appeared at the door.

'Bwana, it's now four o'clock. I have not yet eaten but *yoh*! I have had a good day.'

The mere mention of the word 'eaten' made Daudi yawn again.

Kefa went on, 'I have seen children who would have died or have been blind all their lives made better almost at once by our treatment.'

I interrupted, 'Wait a minute, Kefa. We may have made them more comfortable but there's going to be a week of hard work ahead of us.'

Daudi joined in. 'Truly, Bwana, we must not rest on what we have done. The witchdoctors will be busy.'

Danyeli came in looking exhausted. '*Kah*, Bwana, today has been of no profit at all. Did I not go to the east, to the part of the country where Chikoti has much influence? It was a day of words and words but I have not given out an eye drop or a dose of medicine. We received abuse and heard whispers that trouble is on its way for the hospital.'

I ordered the next day's treatment and then went round the hospital seeing who could be sent home to make room for all the pneumonia children who were coming in. In the Nurses' Quarters I heard the shrill voice of Hilda.

'*Yah!* You know that old woman who scrapes children's throats with her fingernails?' A chorus of grunts apparently indicated that the off-duty nurses did know this sinister old woman who had been directly responsible for a number of deaths.

'Well,' Hilda's voice went on, 'she attacked me. I told Kefa to go away - he's only a man and not very strong in argument. Did I fix her! Oh did I fix her! I said to her, "Do you not come to our hospital when there are pains in your bones? Do you not bring yourself and drink our medicines? Are you not rubbed with our liniment? Do you not use a whining voice and ask for the white pills to take home with you? And yet when we come with our medicines to save the lives of the children you object".' She paused for breath. 'I talked so that the African women would laugh at her.'

The old African matron who, by the way, was Hilda's

grandmother, laughed.

'It's better that people should laugh at her than any other way. If you are rude, they say they are the words of a youngster. If you are angry, people will not listen to you. Truly, you have followed the right path.'

I went on into the ward. There were children in the cots and on the floor, all of them sound asleep, utterly weary after days of being kept forcibly awake. There were a number of glasses of medicine

on the table, under each a slip of paper with the name of the patient who would receive it. Perisi, the nurse in charge of the ward, whispered in my ear.

'I will give them medicine when they wake. Did you not say that sleep is important in pneumonia, for if they do not sleep they will die?'

Coming up the hill to the hospital I saw three little processions. It was the same story in each case – measles, then a cough and then pneumonia. Each child was given an injection and sent off to the ward.

Perisi pointed with her chin to three cots. 'Mubofu brought those sick ones in, Bwana. *Kah*! How he works. He comes and goes like a shadow.'

91

11
An Enemy Spy

The hospital was packed full. Children well on the way to recovery were in our storerooms. Soap, linen, cotton wool and tins of kerosene were at one end piled high from floor to ceiling. The children were not in beds but lying on the floor, each with a blanket and a palm-leaf mat.

On what was usually our verandah, now closed in with great strips of canvas that originally had been part of a safari tent, there were twenty seriously ill little ones lying in beds and improvised cots.

In the wards, to make up for shortness of space, the beds were pushed close together. There was barely room for the nurse to walk between the rows of beds and cots as she made her rounds with eye drops and cough mixture. This yellow, strongly flavoured mixture was highly praised by the crowd of visitors which thronged the place. Many of them were grandmothers who had strong opinions and loud voices.

In the ordinary children's ward with its nine beds

we now had eighteen small patients, four of them extremely ill with pneumonia. We had to resort to the unhospital-like trick of putting two children in one bed. Propped up on pillows they looked at each other across the blankets. The most serious pneumonia cases were in the room where we stored our drugs. In the place where we prayed together a thread-bare blanket tucked over the windows kept the glare away from fourteen children with eye complications.

Checking the list of patients made it clear that many came from distant villages where there were churches and schools. There were those from Manhumbulu where the chief's son had had pneumonia. He had suffered no ill-effects from his midnight trip three weeks before and he was up and running about. To his relations this was little less than miraculous. As a happy result, numbers of people had come to the hospital before pneumonia had had a chance to develop.

It was surprising that we had no less than fifteen patients from the village of Chibaya. They, without exception, had come in as a result of young Mubofu's efforts, which had been helped by the chief's beer party and the considerable hangover which had followed.

Under cover of darkness Mubofu had carried many children in on his back – a six-kilometre journey. He had persuaded some of the bolder women to come themselves and bring their children. He smuggled eye drops and cough mixture to the mothers who were frightened of the chief and told them the story of how and why the children in hospital were recovering. He urged them to let the children sleep and to give them frequent drinks and sweetened gruel, all of which was contrary to custom and the loudly expressed advice of the *waganga*. The blind boy's courage had been notable.

Daudi was coming towards the door. He looked tired out. 'Come in, Daudi, and sit down. Have you had a heavy day?'

'Bwana, the epidemic is not as strong as it was in many places but in others it is much, much worse. *Yoh...*' he sank back in a chair. 'Doctor, it's good to rest.'

'Young Mubofu isn't resting much. It's amazing what that boy is doing.'

Daudi leaned forward. 'It's about him that I came to speak to you. I'm frightened. The village of Chibaya is going to strike back. Things have gone our way for too long. When Mubofu comes tonight with the children he has collected during the day, we should keep him here. I have warnings from Ndogowe that Chikoti knows who is bringing the children here and that he plans mischief. Behold, that evil man is as cunning as a snake. He may not strike now but he has dark plans for the boy and I have fears.'

It was nearly midnight when a whispered '*Hodi*' came at my window. I recognised Mubofu's voice and hurried outside in my pyjamas.

'Two tonight, Bwana.' His voice was full of satisfaction. 'One only has measles. She was able to walk by herself but the other one I had to carry. I heard him grunting as he breathed. Did you not say the other day that this is what people do when they're getting pneumonia?'

'Mubofu, you're becoming quite a doctor yourself.'

There was sheer joy in the sound of his laughter. 'Bwana, I've never been so happy in all my life.'

Together we walked up to the hospital. During the last three weeks he had made that trip nearly every night. More than half the children who had come as a result of those secret safaris would either have died or had permanent damage to their sight if they had been left without hospital care.

Mubofu strode in front of me, certain of every step he took. Uncannily he seemed to know every twist and turn in the path. He held his head high. Somehow our two new cases were squeezed in, then I took the blind boy back with me to my kitchen, gave him a cup of tea and a huge chunk of iced cake.

He tasted it and smiled. 'Bwana, this is wonderful food. It must be on such things that angels live.'

I was amazed at the way in which he had matured in so short a time. I put my hand on his shoulder.

'Do you remember the day we were in the great church at Dodoma when you asked me about heaven and how to get there?'

He nodded. '*Kah*, Bwana. I think many thoughts of God and Jesus and the cross and I thank him for giving me the chance to be useful for him.'

'My thoughts travel the same road. There is great satisfaction in being able to do things for Jesus. I like to remember that he wiped out our sins when he died on the cross so that they are forgiven and forgotten.'

'Why is it, Bwana, that not everybody asks to be forgiven?'

'Consider these sicknesses we're fighting at the moment, Mubofu. There are those who accept the medicines and those who refuse them. There are those who ask Jesus to forgive them their sins and to give them everlasting life in heaven. There are those who turn their backs on him and close their ears to his words. They open their thoughts to the whispering of *shaitan* - the devil, and prefer to be in his family.'

The boy had finished his cake. 'Did Jesus himself talk about this?'

'Oh, yes, he did. He told about the sheep and the goats.'

Mubofu chuckled. 'I know about these things. Do I not go out with those who herd the cattle and the sheep and the goats? Tell me, what did Jesus say?'

'I'll read it to you from God's book. Jesus is talking to those who learnt from him. He said: "When the Son of Man comes in his glory and all the angels with him he will sit on his throne in heavenly glory. All the nations will be gathered before him and he will separate the people one from another as a shepherd separates the sheep from the goats. He will put the sheep on his right and the goats on his left.

'"Then the King will say to those on his right: Come, you who are blessed by my father. Take your inheritance, the kingdom prepared for you since the creation of the world. For I was hungry and you gave me something to eat. I was thirsty and you gave me something to drink. I was a stranger and you invited me in. I needed clothes and you clothed me. I was sick and you looked after me. I was in prison and you came to visit me.

'"Then the righteous will answer him: Lord, when did we see you hungry and feed you, or thirsty and give you something to drink? When did we see you a stranger and invite you in, or needing clothes and clothe you? When did we see you sick or in prison and go to visit you?

'"The King will reply: Whatever you did for one of the least of these brothers of mine you did for me."'

The boy was on his feet. 'Bwana, these are wonderful words. Am I not one of his sheep?'

'You are, Mubofu, and so am I, and it is the most wonderful thing to me in all my life.'

'But you're a doctor and you have much learning.'

'This is a small thing, Mubofu. The thing that matters most is that I am one of his sheep, one of his family, and that my sins are forgiven and forgotten.'

He went to the door and faced the darkness of the night. 'What about the others, Bwana, the ones on his left? What will he say to them?'

'His words are strong ones. He will say: "Go, depart from me. You have no place in my family. You are of the family of *shaitan* - the devil, and will share in his harvest."

'Jesus' own words are: "I tell you the truth. Whatever you did not do for one of the least of these you did not do for me. Then they will go away to eternal punishment, but the righteous to eternal life."'

Mubofu sighed. 'There are many in my village who follow the way of the goats. How are we to teach them God's words?'

'Many have come here these days with sick children.

We will be able to tell the children, their mothers and grandmothers the words of God. God speaks about his words as being seed. We're planting that seed and you are helping us to do it. The harvest does not often come fast.'

He faced round to me. 'It has happened fast for me and that's why I must go back to my village to work for him.'

I stood beside him and, putting my arm round his shoulders, said earnestly, 'We would rather you stayed with us for a while. There is danger at Chibaya.'

The boy slowly shook his head. Abruptly his muscles tensed. He raised a finger and whispered, 'Bwana, quietly. Someone moves out there, someone who does not want to be heard.'

I listened but could hear absolutely nothing.

'There it is, Bwana. I heard him again. He's coming round beside the tank. He's been listening at the window. He's now going away.'

I screwed up an old newspaper and held it to the fire. With it blazing I dashed out into the darkness barely in time to see a figure blending with the shadows of the thornbush not far from the house. My

99

torch burnt out. But for the crickets' song, the whole night seemed to be still. I walked back to the kitchen.

Mubofu crouched in the doorway. He cupped his hand in front of his lips. 'Bwana, there are those who have no joy in the work of the hospital and towards you there is deep anger. It may be they will try to do you harm, to do what will bring you pain.' I remembered what Daudi had said earlier in the day, 'If Chikoti harms the boy, that way he knows he will bring us sadness.'

Mubofu gripped my arm. 'I must return. There is still work for me to do.'

Wishing him good night and Godspeed, with deep apprehension I watched him walk into the ominous darkness of the night.

12
Enemy Attack

Through my head flashed grim pictures of what could happen to my young African friend. I knew something of what witchdoctors could and would do. Sleep would not come. I slid out from under the mosquito net planning to write up all that had happened in those days – to capture the excitement of it, the dangers, the difficulties, the frustrations – but words would not come.

From over the thornbush jungle and the swamp came the eerie rhythm of drums. They beat like a pulse in my aching head. I wrote a few drab sentences, crossed out a word here and there, then re-wrote all of it. But it was still not what I wanted. I tore a sheet of paper out of the writing pad, screwed it up, hurled it into the waste-paper basket and tried again. But the drums were too much. They seemed to taunt me – to jeer, to threaten. The wind had strengthened and I could hear wild singing from Chikoti's village. I shivered and made a further effort.

I wanted others to share our problem, our struggle – to sense a hospital crowded to capacity where we faced shortages of water, of food, of blankets, of linen. Everything was makeshift, shoddy, out-of-date, inadequate.

I tried to express on paper the struggle it was to keep calm with those who thought more of primitive customs than results that stared them in the face. I looked at my battered alarm clock. It said one o'clock. I wasn't in the mood for writing. I wasn't in the mood for sleeping. Action might help.

I lit my hurricane lantern and set out for the hospital, grasping a knobbed stick in case snakes happened to be on the path. I was closing the hospital gate when there was a crash and an outburst of angry voices. The ward was lit up by flames!

There came a chorus of screams. I dashed to the door and forced it open. On the floor, blazing like a giant torch, was one of the palm-leaf mats we used as mattresses. Seizing the non-blazing end I dragged it through the ward, the flame lighting up children's

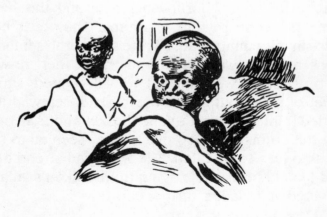

faces peering in terror over the top of blankets. I left it to burn in the courtyard and dashed back into the ward to find out the cause of the trouble and if any damage had been done.

It appeared that an old woman had crept into the children's ward in the late evening. Her grand-daughter lay in bed so drastically ill with pneumonia that she was barely conscious and had a high fever. The old woman picked her up, put her on the floor, calmly went to sleep in the child's bed and covered herself completely with the blanket. There was no outcry.

The night nurse had been in another ward giving treatment to the eye patients and when she came to do her rounds she found the grandmother where the child should have been. She was full of righteous indignation and had dragged the old woman out of the bed. The grandmother resented this treatment and grabbed hold of the bedside locker which had once been a kerosene box. Over went the locker. Over went the lantern, breaking and spilling kerosene onto the mat, which burst into flames.

Firmly I led the old woman outside. She protested that it was against all custom that a child should sleep in a bed and the grandmother on the floor. I told her that it was against our custom that grandmothers should sleep in the ward with the children. I took her to a place where she could sleep and lent her a mat and a blanket.

Back in the ward I found some of the children were still terrified. Others had slept throughout the whole drama. Soon all was quiet again. In one corner of the ward was Mazengo, Chikoti's grandson, the small boy whom Mubofu had brought in. He was critically ill. I gave an injection into a vein but, knowing this was not without risk, I felt it wiser to be close at hand in case of complications.

I went over to my office. Suddenly, it was easy to write. The words flowed from my pen. Page after page was added to a big brown envelope on which was written: Jungle Doctor's Enemies. I yawned and stretched, turned down the lamp and went to the door. The night nurse was rushing towards me.

'Chikoti's men have taken away little Mazengo', she panted. With *pangas* - large knives - they had slashed the mosquito wire of the window and pushed their way in. 'They're fierce men, full of anger. They pushed me onto the floor. I could do nothing to save him.'

I turned up the lantern and searched the hospital grounds. All I found was a gaping hole in the fence. As I gazed at it the drums seemed to beat louder and faster as though Chibaya was celebrating a victory.

The next day was unusually cloudy. Twelve hours of sunlight was usual in our part of the world. Fewer people came that day for medicine. There was less laughter at the hospital.

In the late afternoon Daudi visited me. 'There are those that speak today in whispers. There are rumours – ugly rumours.'

My weary reaction was a shrug of my shoulders. 'I was up more than half the night and have been too tired to take much notice. The old woman started that fire in the ward and then the men slashed a hole in the fence and ran away with young Mazengo…'

Old Sechelela came to the door. 'Come in, grandmother, *Karibu*, Bibi.' I laughed while placing a chair for her.

She sat down and leaned forward. 'You call me grandmother and so I am. And I speak to you as a grandson, one who does not understand as I do the fear that is bred in the hearts of the people by those who are the children of *shaitan* - the devil. Already there are those that say the hospital will be bewitched and a curse will be placed on those who work here and who are treated here.'

'And what is your answer to all this?'

'Shaitan is strong.' She spoke slowly. 'But Jesus is stronger. I have been talking to those who nurse. They have fear as I do. But I told them, "Who fears hyaena when lion is his friend?"'

Daudi's face looked troubled. 'Deep within me is fear also, but I know that God will protect us.'

That night there was ominous quiet: no drums, no singing. It was the stillness that seems to come before storms. I went to bed exhausted and woke at dawn to realise that for the first time in many days I had not heard Mubofu's 'Hodi' in the middle of the night and, just as remarkable, there were no little groups of sick people coming up the path to the hospital that morning.

Daudi was at the door, visibly upset. 'Doctor, truly we have been attacked with witchcraft. Come and see.'

Outside the main gates of the hospital, right across the path was a long line of fine white ash. My assistant stood well back from it.

'It looks harmless enough, Daudi. What does it mean?'

'The witchdoctor from the village where Mubofu lives has cast a spell on the hospital – a spell of strength. Many people are terrified. More than twenty patients have run away. They went through the hole in the fence made by those men when they took young Mazengo. Nobody will walk across that...' he pointed to the line of ashes: 'To cross that they think would mean death.'

'And you, Daudi?'

'I, too, Bwana, walked through that hole but I brought with me this,' and he picked up a broom.

The windows of the ward seemed to be full of faces. Slowly and deliberately Daudi swept the ashes away from the path. It seemed to me I could hear a sigh come from the hospital.

'Daudi, I am going to pray loudly that many may hear. Thank you, God, that you have all power, that you are stronger than *shaitan* and all his works. Thank you that Jesus, your Son, has overcome the devil and taken the sting out of death. Thank you for telling us that if we resist the devil he will run away. That is what we are doing now, almighty Father. Thank you for your hands protecting us, amen.'

Daudi looked at me and deliberately walked through the hospital gate. As I followed him he said, 'Today will be very quiet and difficult because people's hearts are full of fear. They fear spells more than they fear disease.'

We spent considerable time in the wards explaining that there was nothing to fear now. Many of them looked at me as though I were a small child who could not be expected to understand danger when he saw it. Only a handful of people came for medicine instead of the usual hundred, and reports told us that the whole countryside was resounding with a whispering campaign. 'Go to that hospital and you will die' was the grim message being passed from mouth to mouth.

I called the staff together. 'Let me tell you the words of *Mulungu* – Almighty God – whom many of us call Father. Once long ago there were three men who lived in a country where the king did not follow the ways of God. He was full of pride and immensely rich. He had a great golden image made. It was as tall as a buyu tree and broader than an elephant. It was enormous and all of gold. When it towered up in the middle of the city in all its shining magnificence, he ordered that everybody in the whole of his kingdom was to bow down before it when music was made by a band of men who played many musical instruments.

'The three young men, who loved God with all their hearts, prayed to him and told him of their great difficulty. They worshipped God only and they decided that they would not bow down to the king's golden image, even though he had said that anyone who refused to do so would be thrown into a huge fire.

'The great day came. The city was crowded. People stood in awe gazing at the huge golden image. A great fire was lit. The heat of it made people draw back. The musicians played their music and everybody in the whole kingdom bowed down – all except the three young men who stood upright on their feet. People looked at them in amazement. The king himself was full of great wrath. He ordered the three young men to be brought before him and he said, "Bow down to that image." And they said, "No. Our God is the only true God."

'"If you don't bow down to that image," said the king, "I will have you thrown into the great fire."

'But they replied, "Oh, king, we cannot worship your image and we would like you to know clearly and definitely that our God whom we serve is able to deliver us, and he will. But even if he does not, know clearly, oh king, we will not bow down to the golden image."'

In a hushed voice Daudi asked, 'And was their God our God whom we call our Father who is in heaven?'

'He was, Daudi. When the king heard their words he was furious. He ordered the fire to be made seven times hotter and then roared, "Bind them hand and foot and throw them in!"

'All the thousands of people who watched saw them being bound and thrown into the flames. "Behold," they said, "this is the end of those who do not obey the great king who made this golden image." But as they looked, there in the heart of that fire were not three men but four. The king himself looked. He could not believe it. And then, the anger gone from his voice, he said, "Did we not throw in three men? The fourth looks like the Son of God."

'So he called in a loud voice and the three young men walked out of the flames. They weren't even scorched, but the ropes and the strips of clothing that bound them had gone from their hands and legs and the men who threw them into the fire were so badly burned that they died. These are words of truth and, behold, today in our hospital here we are meeting a test. Do we believe in God and serve him like those three young men? Do we believe that our God whom we serve is able to deliver us, and that he will?'

Daudi stood up. 'Bwana doctor, I believe that.'

'And I,' said old Sechelela. 'I believe it with all my heart.'

Some nodded their heads. Others looked this way and that. Many had crowded round.

I stood on a chair that all might hear. 'When you fight it is a good thing to have weapons. Do you remember when Jesus was tempted by *shaitan* - the devil, that he beat him every time with God's book? Listen, here is a verse that we will use in this fight. They are God's words directly to you and they are in the book of Isaiah.

' "Do not fear for I am with you. Do not be dismayed for I am your God. I will help you. Yes, I will uphold you with the right hand of my righteousness."

'Shall we go forward to the attack trusting in him?'

There was a nodding of heads.

'You have seen that Daudi swept away with a broom the medicine that was put around the gate.

Thus we have told *shaitan* that we do not fear him because we trust in God who is stronger. Some of you expected Daudi to be struck dead because he swept the witchdoctor's charm away. Many times we sing, but today let us make music which is a battle song.'

In the tribal language Daudi's voice led:

Fight the good fight with all your might.

Christ is your strength and Christ your right.

They sang it lustily, again and again. As the strains died away I urged, 'Come, we're not going to defend our hospital, we're going to attack!'

13

Manoeuvring

Samson was mending the gap in the fence. 'When you see the paw marks of *simba*, the lion, on the path, Bwana, you…' He looked at me questioningly.

'You suspect lion has passed that way.'

He nodded. 'And when a fence is slashed and when medicine has been spread at the hospital gate – medicine which talks of witchcraft and black magic – you…'

'You think of Chikoti and those who work for him, Samson.'

He wove stout wire into the gap and pulled it tight.

'And this is the first day we have not had a visit from Mubofu for almost a month. Could you find someone who can go to Chibaya without being noticed who could bring us news?'

He paused a moment. 'There are amongst those that we have helped some who will do this. But we must be careful. I will talk with Sechelela. She will know how best to do this.' He picked up his tools and walked off towards the women's ward where we could see Sechelela at work.

The girls' boarding school was situated down the hill from the hospital. There were a number of cases of measles there. All of them were well on the mend, but I feared another outbreak when some thirty girls came back after holidays in faraway villages.

I told the headmistress all that was happening. 'We're having a battle at the hospital and I want your help. Would you call the girls together and see if they will take a hand in the fight?'

It was not long before I looked down on a group of smiling faces. 'Will you help me? There is not room in the hospital for all the children who are sick and I want to have a special ward for those who get what we call infectious diseases, like measles and chicken pox and the cough that whoops. I already have the cement for the floor and Suliman, the Indian trader, has promised to bring me much dried grass for thatching the roof. So you see I have the roof and the floor but I need the material to keep them apart!'

The girls laughed. 'We'll help you to make some mud-bricks, Bwana.'

'Mud-bricks have little strength in the days of rains,' I replied, 'and they take time to make. What I want is stones, not bricks. Would each of you carry a stone a day for me from the river bed so that we can build a ward to help the sick children?'

Nods came from all directions. 'Bwana, indeed we will help. And we will carry more than one stone a day.'

In less than an hour a long line of children looking like a queue on the move was on its way from the river. African women have particular skill in carrying heavy loads balanced on their heads. I was amazed at the size of the pile of stones that had been brought. Women from the village joined in and helped.

A message was sent to our Indian friend and he undertook the next day to send the grass over for the roof. We spent that afternoon busily working out plans.

Through the window I saw little groups of people make their way furtively back to the hospital. A number of those who had run away in the morning were back in time for the evening meal. Like wind through a cornfield the news had spread over the countryside that we had spurned the spell and nothing had happened either to Daudi or myself. More than that, we had set to work to build another ward in the hospital to make space for more sick people.

Shortly after darkness fell a woman whose child had recovered from measles came hurrying up a path that led from the swamp. 'Bwana,' she panted, 'at midday I saw men attacking the blind boy. They hit him many times with sticks. They beat him on the head and on the body till he fell to the ground. I think he's dead, for I saw them throw him into a hole amongst the reeds in the place where hyaena lives with his many relations.'

Immediately we mustered a search party armed with lanterns and torches. Sukuma, crammed to the doors, was pushed down the hill. She sputtered and we drove hectically towards Chikoti's village. In my mind was the picture of slinking hyaenas, afraid to come near a man when he was up and well but only too willing to attack an unconscious boy.

We jerked to a stop at the place where less than a month before the blind boy had led us home through the darkness. Picking up my torch, I ran down a creek, but others were before me. Lanterns dotted the thornbush flat that had been torn about by soil erosion.

Then, from a deep hole beyond a tangle of cactus, Samson shouted, 'Here he is!' He held his lantern high. We forced our way painfully through a tangle of vicious thorny undergrowth.

Daudi stood up. 'His heart still beats, Bwana. But look what they have done to him.'

The boy's face was gashed and his head and shoulders were a mass of ugly bruises. I knelt beside him. 'They've broken his arm and his collarbone and his skull is probably fractured.'

I had sticking plaster and bandages in the emergency kit. 'We'll do the best we can with these fractures but it's his life that matters. Samson, there's a blanket in the back of old Sukuma. Would you please bring it? We must keep him warm and treat his shock.'

By the time Samson returned we had the arm and the collarbone supported. We wrapped him gently in the blanket.

Samson, who was a very big man, said, 'Let me carry him, Bwana. It will be safer than any stretcher.'

Back we trooped in silence. From less than a stone's throw away a hyaena howled and was answered by another of its ugly kind from the edge of the swamp.

'*Yoh*,' muttered Daudi, 'we were only just in time, Bwana.'

We drove back along the rough road as gently as possible. 'Daudi,' I muttered. 'What they did was devilish.'

'*Nghhh*,' agreed Daudi. 'And does not the devil enter into men after they have turned their backs on God?'

Samson leant forward. 'This is not where they will stop the fight, Bwana. They will do worse things. We must watch every move. Let me be both night nurse and watchman. I have a weapon that will bring no joy even to the cunning ones of Chibaya.'

Daudi chuckled softly. 'It is a round stone as big as his fist in a long sock. He calls it a tickler. *Eeeh*!' He rolled his eyes.

At the hospital it was nearly midnight when we carried Mubofu to the small room where we could best look after him. His life hung in the balance.

Feeling utterly weary after the strain and excitement of the day, I knelt beside the operating table and prayed for strength and for wisdom. Daudi joined me and together we prayed for the life of the blind boy who had come so close to martyrdom. The light was dim in the theatre.

As we got up from our knees we saw a face pressed against the glass of the window. It was a face I had not seen before. Daudi flung the door open and we rushed out in time to see a dark figure running fast, disappearing through the open hospital gate through which Mubofu had been carried only a few moments before. It was obvious that Chikoti's spies were about. There was violence in the air.

'Have no worries, Bwana,' said Samson through clenched teeth. 'I shall be here...' (he picked up his tickler) 'with medicine for anyone who tries to force his way in.'

In the morning a weary but smiling Samson assured me, 'The news is good, Bwana. No one came near that door. But the child lies there unconscious.'

'Unconscious, but alive, Samson. Now go and get some sleep. You will be night nurse again this evening.'

Through the gate where the spy had run the night before came a long line of schoolgirls each carrying stones for the building of the new infectious-diseases ward. Scores of people came in for medicine. Many of the children who had been taken away by frightened relations were brought back.

At noon Suliman arrived with a lorry-load of bundles of grass. That grass, two metres in length, skilfully placed, would be the roof of the new ward. There was an easing of tension in the hospital generally. I heard laughter again and people came to look at the growing heap of stones and the pile of grass. A carpenter was busy cutting beams and rafters. Masons were facing the stone while others brought sand and cracked stone for the floor.

The big event of the day was when Mubofu started to mutter that he was thirsty. He was able to take some nourishment and some medicine which would give him a quiet night.

Samson had slept most of the day. 'Bwana, what is the news?'

'The news is good.'

'*Koh*,' he said. 'I have been praying for him. He is a child of courage. Truly, he loves God.' Looking towards the place where we planned to build, he said anxiously, 'If we leave the grass on the ground the white ants will make short work of it. Would it be possible, while it is still light, to place it on the roof of the men's ward? It would keep the place cool and will be safer up there.'

It was a splendid idea. Soon most of the grass, of which there must have been a couple of tons, was neatly stacked on the roof of the men's ward. It was done so quietly that the patients were unaware that anything had happened.

I watched the first stars twinkle out and, pleased with what had been accomplished, said to Daudi and Samson, 'The battle is swinging our way.'

Daudi shook his head doubtfully. 'It may be so but behold, we know that Chikoti is a man full of cunning and I fear that he will attack again.'

'Samson will be on watch again tonight, but perhaps it would be wise if we asked Baruti, the hunter, to guard this part of the hospital in the daytime. He has the courage of a lion.'

'It is a word of wisdom,' said Daudi. 'I will speak to him tonight. He lives over there.' Daudi pointed with his chin in the direction of the rising moon.

Against the night sky we could see the materials prepared for our new ward and as I looked it seemed that the moonlight was playing tricks. 'Surely our pile of stones is higher than it was at sundown?'

Daudi spat. 'That is due to the laziness of one of our water carriers. Instead of carrying the grass round to where it could be put on the roof he dumped his loads there. It would not be safe now to put it on top of the ward because we cannot see.'

'You're right. But I don't think it can come to much damage up there.'

'*Lunji* – perhaps,' said Daudi. And there was an odd tone in his voice.

There was a sound of running feet. It was Samson. 'Bwana doctor, come quickly! It's Mubofu. He has become strange all of a sudden.'

14
Secret Weapon

The small boy was lying in bed with a peculiar, fixed look on his face. It appeared as though he was trying to look for something with his sightless eyes. All the time he kept mumbling the name, 'Mazengo, Mazengo.'

Samson was breathing hard beside me. 'Bwana, you remember the small boy Mubofu brought in days ago, the one who had pneumonia, Chikoti's grandson?'

'The one they kidnapped the other night?'

I put my hand on Mubofu's arm. Consciousness seemed to come back for a moment. 'Bwana,' he gasped, 'perhaps they have taken Mazengo from hospital. Is he not in the chief's place, in the place where they store the corn? Help him, Bwana. Help him.'

Once again he lapsed into delirium but kept muttering all the time, 'Mazengo, Mazengo, Mazengo.' Suddenly, he sat up and screamed in terror.

'Quietly, Mubofu,' I soothed, 'all is well.'

'It isn't, it isn't. Go to Mazengo. Go to Mazengo. You will, Bwana?'

'Yes, I'll go if you'll lie down and rest.'

I poured out a dose of powerful sleep medicine. 'I'll go if you'll drink this.' He drank every drop and then sank back on his bed.

Daudi shook his head. 'Bwana, you're not going at this time of night to that place? Don't do it, Bwana. It's dangerous.'

'I have no choice. It may make all the difference to Mubofu's recovery.'

'Doctor, if you must go, take your *nhuti* – rifle with you.'

'To take any weapon would be to invite a fight. I shall go by myself armed with these.' I showed him a couple of bottles, one filled with grey powder and a larger one, corked, with the letters MS visible across the room.

We walked together to Sukuma but found the poor old car crippled. One of her tyres had been slashed with a sharp knife. Chikoti's spies had been at work again.

There was nothing to do but to go by bicycle, so with an electric torch to light me over the hazardous way, I pedalled down the rough track. All the time I had the sensation of being followed, and when a flock of sleepy birds rose noisily out of a kikuyu tree I realised this was not imagination. I pedalled harder than ever and, coming to a patch of intense darkness, stopped, pulling the bicycle beside me behind the trunk of a baobab tree.

A minute later two tall men, each carrying a spear, ran past me breathing hard. The track was narrow. I grinned with satisfaction and silently pedalled after them in the darkness. It was risky riding. Before long Chikoti's village came into view. By the light of the camp fire I could see in front of me the two men who were supposed to be following me. I shone my torch on their shining backs.

'*Kumbe*,' I remarked, 'behold, we all travel the road tonight.'

They looked at me sheepishly. I smiled. 'It's fitting that you should bear news of my coming to Chief Chikoti. Tell him that the Bwana doctor is here and wishes to have words with him.'

I wheeled the bicycle to a camp fire in the centre of the village and sat down on a three-legged stool brought to me by a woman whom I recognised as one of those who had been coming secretly to get medicine at the hospital.

A tense silence descended on the whole village, punctuated only by the stamp of cattle in the cow yard. Eerily came the wailing note of a night bird. An owl flew low over the fire and the people shrank back.

'Behold,' gasped an old man, '*ituwi* – the owl. Is it not a bird of black magic?'

Without a sound I removed the cork from the big bottle. The penetrating smell of methylated spirits spread everywhere. People sniffed. 'What is that?'

At that moment Chikoti arrived. He appeared most affable. '*Karibu* - come in, Bwana. Why do you come to my village on a bicycle at this hour of the night?'

'Chief, I prefer to come on a bicycle these days when there is much talk of witchcraft and when armed men follow me at night.'

Chikoti spat into the fire. Again the owl flew low overhead.

I spoke loudly, 'Behold, is not *ituwi* busy tonight? Does he not smell witchcraft in the air: have I not come to seek a child who has been taken from the hospital? Should you not have great anger, for he is your grandson, Mazengo? If he does not come back to hospital quickly he will die. His sickness is a severe one and the medicines that he needs are special medicines.'

Chikoti nodded. 'Bwana, it is a bad thing for anyone to take him from the hospital.'

I stood up and took a step towards him. 'It has been done. That is why I have come to your village.' I poured some of the methylated spirits from the bottle into the palm of my hand, took a glowing stick from the fire and lit it. For a couple of seconds my arm seemed on fire. The people started back.

'*Yoh*! Behold, this is not magic. This is knowledge. This is what we can do at the hospital.' I went back and sat down on my stool and waited for a reaction.

Chikoti growled. 'Mazengo is not in my village.'

'Well, where is he?'

'*Magu gwegwe* – I don't know – that is your affair,' replied Chikoti rudely.

'He was taken from the hospital by your men.'

'*Koh!*' He spat. 'You saw them, Bwana? You recognised them?' He turned away.

'Wait.' My voice sounded husky. 'I have evidence that you beat and tried to kill the blind boy.'

Chikoti snarled at me. 'If the relations have anger because their own children are carried off, what is that to me? And as for Mazengo, I know nothing.'

I sprang to my feet. 'Chief, you lie. He is in this village. I know he is here and you yourself shall lead me to the place where he lies.'

Chikoti was trembling with anger. He waved his hand to a group of men seated behind him. They sprang to their feet. Some had spears, others had knobbed sticks – *knobkerries*. I backed away till the fire was between me and Chikoti's bodyguard.

'*Koh!*' I taunted. 'You have proved your lie by your actions.'

I took from my pocket the bottle of grey powder and poured its contents into my right hand. The chief again motioned to his men. They moved towards me.

'Look!' I yelled, pointing with my left hand into the centre of the fire. For a split second they stopped and gazed at the flames. In that moment I threw the handful of grey powder into the heart of the fire, at the same time covering my eyes. The night was split open as the magnesium powder fired.

Chikoti and his thugs fell over each other, dazzled and blinded by the intense light. I grabbed the flabbergasted Chikoti by the arm. 'Take me to him,' I ordered.

Without a word he went across to his own house. There by the light of a kerosene lamp I saw the child lying on a blanket. My fingers on his pulse told me that the chief had unwittingly told the truth. I stood up.

'Chikoti, indeed Mazengo is no longer in your village. He has gone on the last long safari.'

15

Fire!

My heart was heavy as I rode back to towards the hospital. A night bird, dazzled by the light of the torch, flew straight towards me. Swerving to avoid it, I saw something white seeming to beckon me from the thornbush on the side of the road. I dismounted and found the pyjama coat that young Mazengo had worn in the ward. Those who had snatched him from the hospital must have wrenched this from the boy's back and thrown it into the bush.

I wheeled the bicycle over a particularly rough piece of road, mounted again and rode along a flat stretch between two river beds. From the village behind me, a drum started to beat – with a rhythm that was entirely strange to me. It seemed to carry some sinister message. What it was I had no idea, but it made me pedal harder. I thought that if they were prepared to act as they

had with young Mazengo, they may still have plans to injure Mubofu.

Silhouetted on the hill I could see the hospital buildings. It was comforting to see a hurricane lantern moving round from window to window, which told me that the night nurse was on her job.

At the far corner of the fence another lantern was moving. My night watchman was on the spot and prepared for emergencies.

There was still some way to go when, near the place where our new ward was being built, a flame leapt into life. Within seconds, it was a huge blaze. Somebody had set light to the pile of grass piled on the stones for the building. I saw figures rushing from all directions and I knew there was little hope of saving any of that grass. Now I understood the message of the drum.

I forced the old bike along faster than she had ever gone before. Obviously, their next move would be to set fire to the grass on the roof of the hospital ward, the ward where young Mubofu lay, fighting for his life. The shock of a fire at this stage could easily tip the balance against his recovery.

Near the gate, not twenty paces ahead, was a man clinging, lizard-like, to the wall of the hospital. There was the splutter of a match being struck and a tiny flame moved towards the pile of grass on the roof an arm's length away.

I jumped off the bike. With a yell I threw the electric torch. It caught the dark figure in the middle of the back. The match went out. There was a gasp and he fell heavily but in a second he was on his feet and racing past me. I dived at him but collected only a dirty black cloth. Chikoti's man had rubbed the whole of his body with cow fat to make it difficult to catch him in the event of a scuffle. I went after him but he was running like a hare. In the darkness he did not notice the bicycle. He trod in the middle of a wheel, and crashed into the corn.

Daudi and several others had come at top speed to see what was happening, but once again the marauder was on his feet. In the glare of the burning grass beside the new buildings we saw him, his long legs and arms throwing the strangest shadows in the red light. He dashed past the women's ward and the theatre.

'*Yoh*!' yelled Samson. 'Look, Bwana. Look now!'

Suddenly, for no apparent reason, his legs soared into the air. He seemed to travel two metres above ground in a lying position and then crashed, letting out a startled yell.

Daudi was holding his sides and roaring with laughter. 'Bwana, it was the clothes line. It caught him under the chin. He didn't know it was there. *Yoh*! Now we've got him.'

But in no time he was on his feet again running in a frenzy of fear. We watched his scantily clad figure disappearing through thornbush so sharp and long that it would make barbed-wire entanglements feel like velvet. We gazed in silent amazement and then laughed till it hurt to laugh any more.

Daudi wiped the tears from his eyes. '*Koh*, Bwana. It could have been worse. Behold, he only burnt a bit of grass. All that we put on the roof of the ward is safe.'

'Truly, but only just. When I arrived he was striking a match to set it alight and then we'd have been in trouble.'

Samson was anxious to speak. 'I'm glad you've come back. Mubofu has been shouting and muttering…'

I went into the ward. Our young patient was delirious. 'Where's the Bwana?' he shouted. 'Where's the Bwana? Where's the Bwana? Where's Mazengo? What have they done to him?' and then he lifted up his arm as if to ward off a blow.

Beside the bandages where his skin had been slashed I could see the bruises. I put my hand on his shoulder. 'Quietly, Mubofu, quietly…all is well. It is I, the Bwana doctor.'

He gasped. 'Bwana, Bwana, what of Mazengo?'

Daudi had tiptoed to stand beside me. On a tray he had a syringe. I rubbed the boy's arm with a swab of cotton wool and gave the injection. For a moment he was frenzied. He seemed to have the idea that once again Chikoti and his thugs were attacking him. 'Yes,' he screamed. 'It is I. It was I who took the children to the hospital. I who am blind wanted to take them where they could have their eyes saved.' He pushed my hand off his shoulder and fell back exhausted onto the pillow. For a moment I thought his pulse had stopped, then it came back very slowly.

I sat watching him, thinking of all that he had suffered in those past few days. As a background was the hopeless blindness which had left him with two pathetic empty eye sockets. He was probably about fourteen, and had known the suffering of hunger, loneliness and the cruel knowledge of being unwanted. Then, instead of living one long black journey of hopelessness and pain, there had come a new purpose into his life, a new object. He had a goal.

His lips were moving. I bent down close. He was calmer as he whispered huskily, 'Bwana, where is Mazengo, my friend Mazengo?'

'I went to him, Mubofu, and found him in the *kaya* – the chief's house.'

'Is he…is he…?' he put up his good hand to me as he tried to find words to get round the question.

I put my arm round him. 'Mubofu, your friend Mazengo is resting.' The words meant much more in the Chigogo language than they do in English. The blind boy understood.

His battered body shook with sobs. I stayed with him until the injection had taken full effect. I rested him back on the pillows and he slept.

Daudi was standing behind me. He murmured, 'Bwana, I have sadness that all this should have happened to him after he has done so much to try to serve God.'

We moved quietly out of the ward and stood talking together in the shade of the pomegranate tree outside. Its wooden-looking fruit showed dark against the white-washed wall of the ward.

'Daudi, are you feeling that God should protect us from this sort of thing?'

'Yes, doctor, I am.'

'Sometimes he does, but do you remember what Jesus himself said? He warned those who would follow him: The foxes have holes and the birds have nests but the Son of Man has nowhere to lay his head. He warned them, too, that he was travelling a journey which would end at the cross, where he would be killed.

'He told them that the same path would be trodden by some of his followers, which did happen to Peter. James was killed with a sword, and Paul had a dreadful time. If you read 2 Corinthians 11 you will see that he was beaten – five times he received thirty-nine strokes with a whip. Once his enemies threw stones at him till they thought he was dead. He was shipwrecked. He spent a day and night in the ocean. He was bitten by snakes and attacked by robbers. He was hungry and thirsty and finished his life by being beheaded – and he did it all with joy because he loved God.

'Right at the end did he not say, "I have fought the good fight, I have finished the race, I have kept the faith. Now there is in store for me the crown of righteousness which the Lord, the righteous judge, will award to me on that day, but not only to me but also to all who have longed for his appearing".'

Daudi shook his head thoughtfully. 'It's a hard road that we travel.'

'It would be if we travelled it by ourselves, but does Jesus not say, "Behold, I am with you always". Mubofu has been treading this hard road that his Lord trod, Daudi, and the scars that he has are small things when we think of what happened to Jesus.'

Daudi drew in his breath and gripped my arm. 'Doctor, look! In the dispensary.'

I saw nothing but heard the crash of a falling bottle. For the second time that night a dark figure dashed past us into the gloom. There was no purpose in giving chase so we went to the dispensary to see what damage had been done. There was a pungent smell of liniment and the floor was littered with broken glass.

'No one's chest will ever be helped again with that liniment, but the pot of ointment…'

'What sort of ointment was it, Daudi?'

He grinned. 'I believe the man who stole that medicine was the one who set fire to our grass and scratched himself considerably in the thorns. That ointment is the stuff we make from chillies. We use it for a very different purpose from soothing.'

From experience I knew that capsicum ointment burnt like fire and acute pain would be suffered if it were to get into a cut.

'*H-e-e-e...*' chuckled Daudi. 'We will hear stories before long about your very strong witchcraft. Each of his scratches will have its own story to tell.'

16

Confusion

'Your electric torch, doctor?' questioned Daudi.

'It should be outside the ward. Behold, the man with the matches had considerable surprise and little joy when it hit him in the back.'

We found the torch where we expected. It still worked. The glass and bulb were unbroken. In its ray shining on the bicycle I saw broken spokes and an ear ornament made of beads strung on giraffe's hair. It was a neat piece of work. I had never seen one like it.

Next day I showed it to Sechelela. She was most interested. 'There are few people who wear these, Bwana. Behold, there is a man who lives near Chikoti's village, a man about whom there are many words. He is one of fierce anger. More than once his spear has been stained with blood.'

Daudi had much the same to say. 'If we ever meet anyone who has one of these in his ear then we'll know who visited us.'

We were too busy to go any further into the matter. There were injections to be given, chests to be listened to, medicines to be made and a series of delicate eye operations to perform.

At first the children had been frightened of even the eye drops, but this morning when I came into the ward with a little tray loaded with bottles, cotton wool swabs and a dish of sterilised sharpened matchsticks I was greeted cheerfully. There were shouts of 'Mbwuka, Bwana.'

'Mbwuka,' I answered. 'Here I am. Sechelela is with me. She has three big lumps of sugar for those who keep their eyes open best.'

'Koh, Bwana,' said one boy. 'You will need fifteen lumps of sugar for have we not all been practising?'

There were ulcers in the eyes of six of these children, partly from their measles infection and partly from the medicine that the witchdoctor had given previously. I went to each of them in turn, putting a drop of cocaine into their eyes to take away pain, then I filled an eye-dropper with a bright yellow solution. Once again a drop was put into each eye.

The mother of one of the children was standing in the doorway, keenly interested in what was happening. I beckoned her. 'Come, tell me what you see in your daughter's eye.'

She looked carefully but nothing appeared unusual to her. Her child was keen to win one of the coveted lumps of sugar and opened her eye wide.

'Yoh,' said the mother, 'behold, do I not see on the window of her eye...' (which was the picturesque way she had of describing the cornea – the clear part) 'do

I not see a patch of green like grass when it has come from the ground after rain?'

'Truly, you have seen what is there. And does not this medicine show us where there is *chilonda* - an ulcer?'

Taking one of the sharpened matchsticks, I dipped its point, and its point only, into the carbolic solution. I bent over the child. 'Keep your eye still, still as can be.'

It was no easy task to touch every bit of that ulcer with the point of the matchstick. I knew that if I pushed it too far or not far enough – it was all a matter of millimetres – there was the risk of permanent eye damage. There was not a flicker from that small girl nor from any of the others. I turned back the eyelids of some, not a comfortable procedure, and painted the inside of the lids with an antiseptic solution. They all behaved splendidly.

'Behold,' I said, 'I cannot award the three prizes. Everybody was so good.'

There was an outcry. 'Bwana, nothing for anybody?'

'Wrong,' I chuckled. 'Something for everybody.'

'*Heeeh*,' they laughed. 'It is a thing of joy. When can we go out? When can we be out in the sun?'

'Four more days. Four more days with that blanket up while you pretend that it is night in the daytime and then…'

'It will be a time of joy.' I waved and then went to see the progress in the building of the new ward. It was going ahead splendidly. Samson was working as foreman and he was checking that the masons did their work well. He looked at me questioningly.

'It is good, Samson. In a week there will be great rejoicing in this hospital. The wall will be up high enough to put on the roof and also we will be able to send home nearly twenty children – all of them well and strong.'

In the men's ward Mubofu was in a pitiable state. He lay there groaning, delirious. His mind was set on sick children still to be brought into hospital. But he imagined himself bound hand and foot and his mind turned in his delirium to that fateful night when the chief's thugs had tried to end his activities by beating him almost to death. For three days he was unconscious. Severe brain damage had been caused by the murderous attack. There was no improvement until the morning when the carpenters were putting up the rafters for the new ward. His temperature came down. His pulse was steady.

In a weak voice he said, 'Bwana, my head, my head. The noise…the noise.'

Daudi raised his eyebrows. I nodded and he brought a glass of soothing medicine. I put it to Mubofu's lips.

He drank it and muttered, 'Bwana, the drums. Don't you hear those drums?'

'No, Mubofu, I hear no drums. I can hear the hammers of the carpenters putting on the roof of our new ward, but no drums.'

'They are there. They're Chikoti's drums. They're beating. They're telling me that I will die.'

Daudi went outside and came back shaking his head. 'Bwana,' he whispered in my ear, 'there are no drums. There are no drums anywhere.'

'Lie quietly, Mubofu, as quietly as you can. See if you can go to sleep. Behold, the pains in your head will get better.' But he needed more than medicine to ease his pain. Twice I did minor operations called lumbar punctures.

All the grass was removed from the ward roof and taken down to thatch the new building. The blind boy was conscious but restless.

He muttered. 'They're hammering, hammering, Bwana. Can't you stop them?'

'They have finished hammering, Mubofu. They're putting the grass on the roof. There is no noise.'

At that moment a donkey brayed about half a kilometre from the hospital. '*Kah*,' he groaned. 'Did you hear that donkey? Does its noise not go right through my head like a nail?'

But improvement was evident and days at the hospital became less hectic. We had taken down the strips of canvas that turned the verandah into a ward. The children who had been desperately ill were now on the mend and hospital routine was almost back to normal.

I sat in my office reviewing what had happened. We had treated over a thousand cases. Two hundred of them had come to hospital. There were more than seventy children who would have been blinded for life if it had not been for eye treatment. Of those that had come under our care, only six had died.

I knelt and thanked God for the opportunity of working for him in the hospital. How often in my home country had I been told not to attempt missionary activities! Going their own way, the Africans were happy enough, it was said. I would like to have had those people with me to experience those hectic weeks. I thanked God for young Mubofu, for what he had done at such tremendous cost to save life and suffering.

As I got up from my knees the blind boy came to the door, his hands over his ears. 'Bwana, can I go somewhere away from the ward where the noises are not so great?' His voice shook. 'Behold, it was no joy to be blind but now when it is pain to hear…' he shook his head backwards and forwards.

I put my arm round his shoulder and took him to a little grass-thatched hut outside the hospital grounds. 'Come, Mubofu, sit down here where it is quieter. Behold, the roof is cool and here the noises will not be so great.'

He sank down on the stool that I had put out for him. He sighed contentedly. 'Yes, it's quieter here. And I cannot hear those drums.'

Speaking softly I told him of the thousand people we had treated for measles and reminded him that twenty-four had come to hospital solely because of his efforts.

'But, Bwana,' he shook his head, 'Mazengo died – my friend Mazengo.'

'Truly, but twenty-three others are now well and they would not have lived if you had not been there.'

For the first time in days I saw him smile. '*Koh*, Bwana, I hadn't thought of that.'

'And then, Mubofu, Mazengo heard the words of God. You told him.'

'Truly, Bwana, I told him and did he not talk to Jesus with me? Is that not why I miss him so much? He was my friend. He understood me.'

'Mubofu, our life in this world will not be very long. It may be many years, it may only be days, but when we set out on our last great safari, behold, we shall see our Lord and receive from him a smile of welcome and hear him say, "Well done".'

'*Heheeh*,' agreed the blind boy as we walked together back to the ward. 'Bwana, there are many pains but, behold, things can come from pain that are worth having.'

'Truly, and did not Jesus himself say that unless a grain of wheat falls into the ground and dies it remains what it is, a single grain. But if it dies it produces many grains. Jesus went on to say that he who loves his life shall lose it, and he who makes his life of no account in this world will keep it for eternal life.'

Mubofu nodded. 'I understand that, Bwana. Yes, now I understand.'

17
Snake Interlude

The move away from the bustle of hospital routine had a good effect on Mubofu, although he still complained of pains in his head. I took him to the new ward when it was finished.

'*Yoh*,' asked Mubofu, 'is there anyone in the ward?'

'No, not yet. But it may be that some girls from the school may become ill when they return from holidays. Even now the germs may be breeding inside them.'

'This measles is surely a bad trouble', Mubofu said as he felt his way round the room. He tested the walls. He ran his hand over the newly concreted floor. He smiled. 'It has a good smell, Bwana.'

'If it had not been for you, Mubofu, we would not have built this ward. Chikoti would not have had a spell put outside the hospital. The stones would still be on the hillside, the grass in the swamp and the timber in the forest, but, instead, we have a special place to fight disease.'

Each morning, when the people of the ward woke up, Mubofu would wrap his blanket round him, go quietly down to the hut outside the hospital wall and stay there resting, gradually convalescing. Noise upset him most, but it was encouraging that he developed an appetite.

Life became busy again at the hospital when fresh cases of measles broke out amongst the schoolgirls. Our new ward was full, but I usually managed to spare ten minutes or so in the middle of the day to go down to Mubofu's little hut and have a chat with him and tell him the news of the day.

One day I brought on two enamel plates a pile of native porridge and cooked beans. He bowed his head and thanked God before he started to eat. While he did so I told him, 'Mubofu, the sick ones are doing well in the new ward – your ward. Although I don't think that you would like to be there because – *hoh!* do they chatter! No one there is in danger now. To save so many from suffering, pain and blindness is work that brings satisfaction right down to the bottom of our hearts.'

Mubofu nodded. 'Indeed. Perhaps when I am better you may be able to find work for me to do at the hospital. I could sweep things and clean things.'

'We will talk of these matters when your headaches are completely better.'

He beamed. 'These days I am feeling much better. My heart sings. To work for God is to have joy.'

As I walked back to the hospital Mhutila, the water carrier and gardener, presented me with a collection of snakes' eggs that he had dug up. I took one of these in my left hand and gave my right to Mubofu. I led him along the path to the new ward, which was almost full of schoolgirls convalescing from measles.

'Would you like to hear the story of this ward, Mubofu?'

'*Heeh*, Bwana, how I would like to hear it, with all the little bits as well.'

'Behold, many of the children of the school and of the village set to work to help me. They walked to the river and carried back many stones. In a few days time there was a large pile, and in two weeks all that we required had been brought. Then there was measuring of sand and cement to be done, and cracking of stones before the foundations were put in.'

When we reached the door of the ward, Mubofu hung back, but I drew him into the ward. Turning to the girls I said, 'Do you remember the day that the foundations were put in?'

'Oh, yes, Bwana,' came a chorus. 'We remember.'

'Well, tell me, what are the foundations for?'

'If you haven't any foundations, Bwana, the building falls down.'

'But why?'

'Because the rains come and wash away the earth at the bottom and the winds come and blow the earth away from the bottom and the walls fall in and the roof falls down.'

For a full minute there was silence while this sank in. Then I asked, 'Are you sure?'

'Yes, we're quite sure.'

'*Kabisa*'

'Yes, *kabisa*.'

'All right then. Now answer me this. Are snakes poisonous?'

'Yes, Bwana, very poisonous.'

'Are little snakes as poisonous as big snakes?'

'*Hongo*, Bwana,' said Mubofu, 'is it not the nature of snakes to be poisonous?'

'Right. Then listen to my story. Sin is like poison. It poisons your soul. Little sins are as dangerous as big sins. Behold I will show you this in a way today that will make it hard for you to forget.'

I put the soft-shelled egg into Mubofu's hand. 'What is this?' he felt it and, with a shudder, dropped it. '*Yoh*, a snake laid that.'

'True.' I picked it up. The sick children's eyes nearly popped out of their heads when I took the egg and put it on a large stone in the middle of the ward. 'Now you're sure what this is?'

'*Eheh*, Bwana, a snake's egg.'

'Oh…and can a snake's egg bite you?'

'No, Bwana, the snake is too little. He is still inside the egg.'

'But, Bwana,' broke in Mubofu, 'if he comes out of the egg, then he could bite you.'

'Truly. So what should I do?'

'Break the egg, Bwana, and the snake will not grow and nobody will be killed.'

'Right, those are words of wisdom.'

Taking a piece of firewood I thumped the egg heartily, sending a most unsavoury collection of rubbish spraying all over the ward. Heads disappeared under blankets like magic.

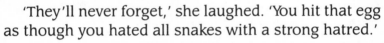

The ward nurse was upset. 'Bwana, you've made a dreadful mess.'

'You're right, but I'll help you clean up. Do you think any of us will forget about the danger of snakes?'

'They'll never forget,' she laughed. 'You hit that egg as though you hated all snakes with a strong hatred.'

'That's the picture I wanted to leave in your minds. There is poison in the fangs of a snake and sin is poison. I hate sin because it kills souls. So let us deal with sins while they are little or they will grow.'

'But, Bwana,' insisted Mubofu, 'we can't deal with sin. Only Jesus can do that.'

'Truly,' I agreed. 'And when Jesus has forgiven your sin, don't forget that it's all-important to build on the right foundation.'

Mubofu walked off happily to his 'house of quietness', as he called it, and I left him to go into the operating theatre.

Two hours later I saw Daudi coming out of the dispensary. 'Would you mind going and bringing Mubofu back, Daudi? It's time he went to bed. It's getting quite dark now.'

'He generally comes back himself before now, doctor. Perhaps he's gone to sleep.'

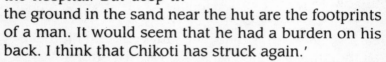

But a quarter of an hour later Daudi was at my door. 'There's no sign of him,' he panted. 'He's not in his hut and he's nowhere near it. We've searched everywhere near the hospital. But deep in the ground in the sand near the hut are the footprints of a man. It would seem that he had a burden on his back. I think that Chikoti has struck again.'

We continued the search but no sign or trace of Mubofu could be found anywhere. He had disappeared completely. I was haunted by the picture I had seen of that huddled-up figure, beaten and left in that dry river bed for the hyaenas and vultures and jackals.

Throughout the night we searched, going all over the country. We had teachers enquiring in the villages. Ndogowe, the donkey man, had no news to bring from Chikito's village. Mubofu's disappearance was a complete mystery.

Always we kept asking the same question of anyone who came in from a distance, 'Have you heard of a blind boy called Mubofu? Behold, he has disappeared.' And always came the same reply, 'Not as yet.'

18

Battle Climax

A week of suspense crept by.

The verandah of our dispensary was crowded with people waiting for treatment. There was an undercurrent of whispering and excited discussion of symptoms.

It was the peak hour of outpatient activity. I was listening to a small girl's chest with my stethoscope when abruptly a loud insistent voice came through the window, 'Bwana, Bwana…'

The voice came from a tall man dressed in a black cloth with red mud in his hair, his earlobes pierced so that a tennis ball could have easily fitted into the lobes.

'Bwana,' he shouted, 'it's a case of a broken leg.'

'Wait a minute,' I answered, as I wrote on a card the treatment the small girl should have. She grimaced as she drank from a medicine glass. To the nurse I said, 'Perisi, would you please call Daudi?'

My assistant was busy examining blood slides for malaria. He came across to me from the laboratory.

'Daudi, there's a man here who says that in his village there's a case with a broken leg which can't of course be expected to walk in. Would you carry on here and see the out-patients who have ordinary illnesses? I'll check through them to see if there is anybody who is very sick and you can give out all the other medicines.' Daudi put on his apron and prepared to do the job.

I looked through the sixty-odd people who were still waiting. Three or four were obviously suffering from acute malaria. I outlined the treatment for a small boy with an ulcer as large as his hand. Squatting in the shade was an old man needing an operation whom I arranged should be admitted.

Then, picking up my hat and a bag that Samson had packed, I prepared to go to the broken leg case. I checked the bag's contents. There were rolls of plaster-of-paris, surgical instruments, a box with an emergency injection kit, some very ancient scissors, a hacksaw blade and an old pair of secateurs I used for cutting plaster.

I turned to the man who was standing beside me impatiently. 'What is your name?'

'They call me Nyama.'

'Tell me, Nyama, where is the break?' I pointed first to my thigh.

'No, not there, Bwana. It is...' He indicated a place

mid-way between his knee and ankle.

'Right, now tell me, has the bone come through the skin?'

'*Hongo*,' said Daudi, 'Bwana, you're asking him if it's a simple or a compound fracture.'

'Yes, that is exactly what I'm asking.'

'*Kumbe*,' said the man, 'behold the skin is in order.'

'Splendid. We'll be alright, Daudi, with this kit. But I'd better take a rubber strip to put inside the plaster. It will be easier to take off later on.'

Daudi took me aside as I was departing and whispered, 'Bwana, I think there is something odd about this. I smell trouble.'

I wondered myself as I replied, 'I hope all will be well. There are too many demands here for you to come with me.'

So I started out on the twelve kilometre walk over the hills. It was quicker to go on foot than by any other means. My guide strode along at a great rate. We passed over riverbeds which were full of moist sand and pools of muddy water where small children were playing, having a glorious time splashing, during those few days in the year when water was available.

Towards a line of hills was a wide sweep of reeds. A flock of ducks swept into the air. 'What is that place over there?' I asked.

Nyama mumbled something vague about *mwiko* – forbidden – but was unwilling to say more. He quickened his pace, making no attempt to answer. I stopped to gaze at this group of hills dotted with huge granite boulders that looked like the ugly teeth of a crocodile.

'Bwana,' urged my companion, 'this is a safari that requires haste.'

'Your legs are longer than mine,' I retorted, 'and there is more breath in your chest.'

Grudgingly he slowed down and at long last the village came into view. It was a meagre group of squat mud-and-wattle houses. We came to one of these *kayas* and I followed my guide through a narrow doorway into the dark interior, where an open fire burning under a porridge pot was the only lighting. By its flickering flame I saw my patient.

Although used to strange sights and peculiar smells, this time I was completely taken aback. There was no doubt that a broken leg confronted me but it was not, as I had unhesitatingly assumed, the limb of a small child but the foreleg of a calf.

I swung round to the man who had deceived me into this long foot-safari. '*Kah*, you bring me all this way in the hot sun leaving the sick people of the hospital and call me away out here to mend the broken leg of a calf?'

'*Heh*,' protested Nyama, 'if you believed a child was suffering you would come. I knew this. But if I had said it was a calf you would have refused.'

'You speak truly,' I answered hotly. 'I would not

have come. Is it my work to look after cattle?'

'Bwana,' he spread his hands wide, 'it is the child of a valuable cow.'

I walked to the door. 'And what about all the sick people at the hospital?'

He shrugged. 'I needed your help.'

Cows are an African's riches. I stood with my hands on my hips, not trusting myself to speak and then it came to me that here I might get news of Mubofu. There was a long, uncomfortable pause, then, lowering my voice, 'I will agree to help you but only if you tell me news of the blind boy who has disappeared from the hospital. No news – no medicine for the cow's child.'

He drew in his breath sharply. There was fear in his eyes. Through the doorway I could see a man with a peculiar ornament in one ear only. I realised, I had seen its fellow on the night of the fire!

I noticed that the man was limping and wondered if the bicycle spokes, the clothes line or the ointment he had stolen had caused the damage!

Nyama looked at me furtively and said, 'Bwana, there is a place of many reeds at the bottom of the hills where you stopped. It is a place that we fear. Those who live round here are forbidden to go there. Perhaps the boy is there.'

'You will show me the way when I have finished mending this leg. Should your memory suddenly fail you there will be *tabu sana* – great trouble.'

'*Koh*, Bwana I would not deceive you.'

'No?' I questioned. 'It is not your habit to deceive people? Have I not found that out already?'

I unpacked my instruments. 'Call your family. Hold that calf still.' And so, with his relations sitting forcibly on the unfortunate calf, I managed to get the broken bones into alignment and to put on a plaster in the approved fashion. There was much amazed comment from the crowd of people who watched. They were not impressed by the gauze covered with plaster-of-paris which they mistook for flour.

'*Yoh*,' came a voice. 'There is small wisdom in doing what he is doing.'

'*Koh*,' growled an old man, 'he ties a piece of cloth around the leg of a creature of strength.'

I moulded the plaster into place, held it there for a couple of minutes, then, seeing that there was some plaster-of-paris still left in the tin, I mixed it up with water and made a small pyramid about as long as my thumb, shaped it and put it on a stone in the sun.

'*Heeh*,' said the old man, 'what does he do now? Is this a charm?'

I could feel the plaster setting on the calf's leg underneath my hands. 'Nyama,' I said, 'it is not a charm. It is a thing of wisdom, a thing that perhaps will make it clear to your mind and your hand that the medicines of the hospital have strength.'

The old man spat. 'Flour has no strength.'

I interrupted him, 'But you have, eh?' He nodded. 'Then see that lump I have shaped? If you were to strike that with the palm of your hand could you crush it?'

There was scorn in his laughter. '*Eheh*, I could.'

'Well, do so.'

He brought his hand down with a hearty whack. The plaster had hardened. '*Yoh*,' he gasped, 'it has the hardness of a stone.' He blew on his palm. '*Yoh*, this is a thing of witchcraft.'

'Ah, no.' I laughed. 'It is a thing of wisdom. See, the leg of the calf now is held so that the bones do not break. The calf can walk.'

The calf was on its four legs, limping a little but moving quite briskly towards its fellows in the cow yard.

'*Yoh*,' said Nyama, 'this is a thing that we have not seen before.'

'Truly,' I replied.

Nyama urged me to stay for a meal of *ugali* – porridge. Thankfully, I agreed. Water was being poured over my hands when I saw Daudi arrive sweating profusely. He greeted the people in the local language and then, speaking to me in English, 'Bwana, I finished the work at the hospital and I knew that there was trouble in this safari so I came to be with you.'

'Thank you, Daudi. There is much trouble here. Did you realise it was a calf's leg that had been broken?'

His eyes opened wide. '*Yoh!* They deceived us all right.'

'That is true, but we have a clue that may help us to find our lost friend. But first let us eat.'

The people were impressed that I was able to eat their food in their traditional way. They watched with approval as I took a handful of the dry native porridge, dipped it into a bowl of boiled beans and ate with noisy appreciation.

'*Yoh,*' chuckled Nyama. 'Has he not learnt well?'

When the meal was finished I took him aside. 'Tell me what you promised. I have kept my part of the bargain. Now tell me truthfully.'

With Daudi in front, he walked down the path and I followed. When we were out of earshot he said, 'In the swamp, in the middle of the lake below those hills you may find the one you seek.' He pointed hurriedly with his chin to the south. He said, '*Kwaheri*', and hurried back the way he had come.

Daudi gripped my arm. 'Come behind this buyu tree, Bwana. Someone approaches.' Peering round the trunk of the great tree, we saw the man with the earring come out of a thornbush thicket and limp along the path that we had just traversed.

'*Yoh,*' muttered Daudi, 'did you notice that his legs, up to his knees, were covered with thick black mud?'

Daudi nodded. 'That is the sort of place where they could hide Mubofu and no one would know anything about it.'

'*Eheh,*' I agreed, 'and the man with one earring is undoubtedly the person who set fire to the grass at the hospital. Judging by the mud on his legs, it could well be that he has the boy there a prisoner.'

'I fear maybe he is more than a prisoner...' Daudi stopped in the middle of the sentence and shook his head.

We pushed on in silence, forcing our way through a thick bed of reeds until we came to the edge of a lake of mud. Daudi prodded carefully with his stick before we waded into it. Every step forward he tested. I took off my shoes and socks and followed him in. We waded for perhaps a hundred paces then suddenly Daudi's probing stick disappeared.

We moved on, carefully avoiding deep mudholes, and at last came to a place where the bottom was solid. We followed this ridge round the edge of an island fenced in by dense thornbush. When a narrow gap appeared we pushed our way through matted reeds and stinking, stagnant water.

Daudi suddenly sprang back in alarm. On the bank were a collection of human bones. Beside them, dried in the hard mud, were hyaena paw-marks. Under a cactus was the unsavoury sight of the rotting body of a vulture. Other birds of prey hovered overhead.

'Koh,' muttered Daudi, 'this is an evil place. See those birds? They expect more death.'

At that moment we saw the house. It was the ordinary mud-and-wattle affair but it had been allowed to fall into ruins. The mud walls were cracked. The roof sagged ominously. Standing in the doorway, inside I could see a figure lying on a tattered blanket.

'Hodi,' I called, 'may I come in?'

From the shadows came a weak, husky voice. 'Bwana.'

'Mubofu,' I cried. ' We have found you at last!'

'Do not come near to me, Bwana.' The boy struggled to sit up. 'I have a great sickness. Keep away.'

My eyes became used to the dim light and I could see Mubofu looking gaunt and haggard. An exclamation came from Daudi. The boy was covered from head to foot with small lumps! I struck a match and in a moment the matter was clear. He had smallpox.

I bent down and felt his pulse. 'Bwana,' he pleaded, 'do not touch me. I have a disease that spreads like fire.'

'I have no fear of it, Mubofu, none at all. Do you remember the scars on my arms? Did I not tell you of the calf that had set me free from this disease?'

Weakly he nodded his head. 'So it's that, Bwana? There was another man here that had the disease. Those of my village heard that he was here so they brought me to the same place. He went outside two days ago shouting strange words and I have not seen him since.' So that was the explanation for the human bones we had seen in the reeds.

Mubofu was pitifully weak. He rested back on my arm, his voice little louder than a whisper, 'Bwana, you told me that in heaven I would see Jesus face to face.'

'Yes, Mubofu. Does it not say in God's own book, "They shall see his face and his name shall be in their foreheads?'

'But, Bwana, will he look at me covered with these?'

He ran his finger over the pock-marks.

'That will all change, my friend, when you pass through the gates. Behold, there are no diseases in heaven and the only scars that are there, Mubofu, are the scars in his hands and his feet and side.'

'*Eeeh*, Bwana, if I had had the scars on my arm like you I would not have caught this disease.'

I held my water bottle to his lips. He leant against me. 'The scars that matter to me are Jesus' scars.'

'That is true, Mubofu. In God's book does it not say that the punishment for our sins is upon him and by his scars we are healed?'

'Bwana, oh Bwana, I so wanted to tell others about him.' He put his hand on mine and sank back on the tattered blanket.

Through a crack in the mud wall a shaft of sunlight lit up his face. The grim work of disease and the witchdoctor was forgotten. There was a calmness and peace on his face which told its own story.

Putting his hand on my arm, Daudi said in a hushed voice, 'Bwana, he is seeing now.'

SAMPLE CHAPTERS FROM:
JUNGLE DOCTOR'S
Crooked Dealings

1
Hunchback of the Jungle

The flames of the camp fire threw huge shadows on the walls of the jungle hospital.

From the dispensary door I could see young Goha. He stood in the background, but his deformed face and the unsightly lumps on his back were clearly visible.

Daudi whispered, 'How long before we can do his operations, Bwana?'

'Everything depends on how he responds to the new medicines. Mosquitoes have done much harm to his blood.'

Lying at Goha's feet was Seko, his small dog, who seemed to have the ability to smile.

Daudi gripped my elbow. 'Look at that dog, doctor.'

Seko's ears were flat. He trembled all over.

'Seko, come here!' ordered Goha, but instead of obeying the dog tried to creep under a three-legged stool.

Goha put one hand over the twisted side of his face and moved forward to pick up the little animal.

It all happened in a second. A brown, hunched-up shadow came rocketing out of the darkness. Snarling, it grabbed the small dog by the scruff of the neck and shot off again into the gloom of the night.

Daudi jumped to his feet. '*Mbisi* - the hyaena! Quickly, after the brute!'

I snatched up my torch. Its beam followed the sound of the little dog's howling as I swept the corn garden systematically with light.

'Save him, Bwana!' gasped Goha as we dashed through the gate.

A muffled howl came from the path ahead as the

beam of light picked out the hyaena trying to swerve round a tall man carrying a knobbed stick.

Thump! The club whacked into the jungle scavenger's ribs. A second wallop caught the hyaena where his tail joined his hunched back. With a yelp he disappeared in the direction of the jungle.

Goha picked up the small dog, who lay huddled beside the path. He ran back and gently put him into my arms. Tears ran down Goha's face.

I examined the dog. One leg was broken, and the teeth of the hyaena had torn him savagely.

In an undertone I said to my medical assistant, 'Daudi, he is so badly hurt that the kindest thing to do would be to help him join his ancestors.'

'*Eheh*,' he agreed.

Goha stood up and came towards me. There was a tragic look on his small face. The sweat on his forehead stood out in beads. 'Bwana, you won't let Seko die?'

'It might be kinder if we saved him from suffering.'

'Seko's brave, Bwana. Please save his life.'

'I'll do what I can. Mboga, take Goha and see that he rests quietly in bed.'

The male nurse smiled. 'Yes, Bwana.'

I put my hand on the boy's shoulder. 'I'll operate, and when we're finished I'll tell you all about it.'

The sick boy looked longingly at his dog, who made a feeble effort to lick his hand.

'We will need penicillin to save Seko,' said Daudi anxiously, 'but in a hospital like this where we are always short of drugs, what can we do?'

'Bwana,' urged Mboga, 'the dog means much to the boy. If Seko dies, Goha will fret. We're not just fighting for the dog's life. Let's do all we can.'

'We will, but I've only operated on a dog once before.'

'*Kah*!' muttered Daudi as he started the primus stove. 'It is a new work, boiling up instruments for an operation on a dog.'

I injected anaesthetic into the little creature, scrubbed up my hands, and set to work.

It was complicated surgery. After an hour Seko, heavily bandaged and with one leg in plaster, lay in a padded box. Mboga carried the small dog to the ward where the glimmer of a lantern showed that Goha was still awake.

Daudi went in. 'The Bwana worked with skill. His hand was as gentle for the dog as it will be for you.'

'*Eheh*,' nodded Goha, 'of course.'

'He also gave injections of penicillin, for the teeth of hyaena are covered with *vidudu* - germs.'

The boy asked hoarsely, 'Bwana, what is news of my dog?'

'He's sick, very sick. Do you want me to tell you exactly what I think?' He nodded. 'The chance for him to recover is small.'

Tears rolled down his face. 'Bwana, you did everything you could?'

'Yes, everything.'

He lay there quietly for a while and then, 'Does God listen when we pray for dogs?'

'Yes, Goha, he does. But we can't tell God what to do. He knows best. Often he is answering before we ask. You see, there would have been no hope for Seko unless that tall man with the knobbed stick had been on the path. Also, he would certainly have died if we hadn't operated at once. It isn't only a matter of his neck and leg, but the teeth of hyaena have torn him deeply inside.'

'What have you done, Bwana?'

'I have fixed everything up, but it was not easy. I have also set and splinted his left leg. It was not only broken but it was crushed. Seko will have much pain.'

'Bwana, for a year Seko has been my only friend.'

'We know these things, Goha, so we have done the best we could.'

The boy climbed out of bed and quietly knelt down.

2

The Man with the Twisted Face

The drums throbbed in the village as I walked under the pepper trees. A hand came out of the darkness. Startled I swung round, and a deep voice boomed, 'Bwana, it is I, Nusu, who have come to greet you.'

I held up my hurricane lantern and peered into a face half covered by a huge hand.

'Remember me, Bwana?'

'*Kah*! How could I forget the man with the twisted face?'

He laughed and removed his hand to show a broad smile on a normal face.

'I came to greet you, Bwana, but a hyaena with a dog in its mouth ran into my leg. I thumped it with my knobbed stick.'

'*Yoh*, Nusu, you have done an important thing for a boy and his dog. You, and only you, can help him in another special matter. Tomorrow will you come at the time of the morning drum?'

At dawn an urgent voice sounded outside the mosquito-proof wire of the window of my bedroom.

'Bwana!'

'What's up?'

I recognised the voice of Wendwa, the night nurse. 'It's young Goha. His temperature is 41°.'

'I'll come at once.'

I dressed rapidly and ran with my mind asking, what could have caused that wild rise?

I tiptoed into the ward and took Goha's pulse. It was normal. His forehead was cool.

'Let me see the thermometer, Wendwa.'

It read 41°, but the mercury wouldn't shake down. She raised her eyebrows.

'Let's try another one.' I checked it, put it under Goha's arm and kept it there for three minutes.

His temperature was 37° - perfectly and beautifully normal.

'Bwana,' whispered the night nurse, 'I'm sorry. I thought you ought to know at once. I didn't wait to try another thermometer.'

'You were right. I'm only thankful he doesn't have a high fever like that. While I'm here, how's that small dog?'

'Asleep, Bwana.'

Daudi appeared in the doorway. 'What's happening, doctor?'

'A false alarm. I was told Goha's temperature was way up but it was only the thermometer that had fever, not the boy.'

Daudi grinned. 'How's the smiling dog?'

We hardly dared to look into the box where he lay. When we did, two brown eyes looked up and a curly tail wagged feebly.

'He's alive and better than seemed possible,' I breathed. Goha awoke and eagerly bent down to look at his dog. His eyes were glistening. 'Bwana, Seko's much better.'

'*Yoh!*' agreed Daudi. 'Surely it is a thing of thankfulness about the little dog.'

Goha broke in. 'Off and on all night I have been asking God to help him.'

'Would it not be good now to thank him?'

We did.

A drum started to beat.

'*Yoh*,' smiled Daudi as Nusu joined us. 'An old friend has arrived. And you, Mboga have a story of high interest for Goha.'

'Truly. I had just started working at the hospital two years ago and Nusu came with a banana leaf covering half his face. With this in place he looked normal. But when you saw the other side, *koh*! How twisted it was. His eye was lower on the right side than the left and the corner of his mouth seemed to go up and meet it.'

Goha spoke softly, '*Kumbe*! You were almost as I am?'

They stood looking at each other for a while then both smiled. The boy's face was distorted.

'*Yoh*, Great One, the Bwana worked well on your face.'

'*Eheh*! He will do the same for you also.'

Goha started to ask questions. I left them talking together.

As we worked that afternoon, Daudi pointed to Goha and Nusu sitting under the buyu tree. 'There is good work going on there, doctor. That Nusu has truly become one of God's family. *Hongo*, my heart feels warm to hear him tell what is happening in his life.'

'Truly, Daudi. I'm looking forward to hearing him tell his story tonight.'

A little while after sunset, I heard cheerful singing round the camp fire as I visited the ward. Seko was certainly holding his own. Goha, as usual, had half his face covered with his hand.

'Come with me, Goha, and join the singing.'

As we sat by the fire, Nusu took up his drum and we sang one of the tribal responsive songs.

'Tell us about your trouble and its cure now, Nusu.'

'*Eheh*, Bwana.' He stirred up the fire. 'Behold, I had heard many stories of the work of your medicine here. There was a child who had a large ulcer on her

face and you cured it, and then an old man who had no joy in his stomach. *Kumbe*, you treated it with success and he sang your praises strongly. It was a thing of wonder in our village. I heard these words and many more, Bwana, while I sat in the darkness of my house, for I feared to go outside.'

'I came at night, for there was no joy in eyes that looked curiously at me. You examined me and asked many questions. Then you said, "*Kumbe*! I can fix that up for you. In a moment I will get a bandage and cover that side of your face."

'Your words brought small joy, for covering my face did not cure the trouble. But you were the doctor so I agreed and Wendwa put on a bandage. I looked at myself in the mirror. *Yoh*! If only both sides had looked like that!'

'Wait a bit, Nusu,' I interrupted. 'Before you went home that evening

I called Daudi and Wendwa aside. You know our habit here each day is to ask God to guide us in all we do. We prayed together and then I told them, "This man's case is beyond me. I have never seen anyone like him. I'm not sure what the cause of his trouble is. Let us ask God to help because it says in the book written by James, "If any of you lacks wisdom let him ask God."

'Later I took through my surgical books with care. For hours I read, and when I put the last one back on the shelf I still had no idea what to do.'

'Had you no more books, Bwana?' asked Goha.

'None, but on the table was a copy of the Medical Journal that had arrived in the mail that afternoon. I tore off the wrapping and turned over the pages. Suddenly my eyes opened wide. There was an article on the very thing I was looking for. There in front of me was a picture of a man exactly like you, Nusu. Underneath the photo were all the details of how to do that operation. But this was small comfort, for it said clearly that it was only to be undertaken by the experienced.'

Daudi took up the tale. '*Kumbe*, doctor! To those of us who help you it was a thing of wonder, and Nusu here drew in his breath to see the pictures in that journal.'

Nusu laughed. 'Bwana, if your face had been twisted like mine you would have had deep interest, too, in that *gazetti* with its photographs.'

'*Hongo*, Nusu! Your eyes really stuck out when I showed you those before and after pictures. But you remember I explained that it was no easy task ahead of us. We were ready to do our best but couldn't be sure that the result would be all that you expected or we hoped.'

'Bwana, I put myself in your hands.'

Daudi broke in. 'That was faith. The doctor told you that perhaps he could help. Surely we do a much safer thing when we put our lives into God's hands. Did not Jesus say, "Come unto me and I will give you rest?" There's nothing of the perhaps about that.'

Nusu smiled. 'It took me a while to understand that, but I do now. The night before you worked I had many doubts. Sleep was hard to catch, but Daudi came with a yellow pill and at dawn you operated.'

'Wait a bit, Nusu. How do you think the doctor feels the night before?'

'*Magu* - I don't know.'

'I felt unhappy. The work was beyond me so I turned over the pages of my Bible and found the words, "I the Lord God will be your confidence". That made me feel better about the operation.'

· Nusu nodded.

'What I was looking for was a little piece of gristly tissue that was growing in the wrong place and pulling both your eye and mouth out of place. It was no easy work to do. Anyway, after about half-an-hour, from underneath your eye I removed a swelling the size of the last joint of my thumb. It was tucked away and stuck down deep to the skin and bone, anchoring each in an unnatural position. The last few minutes were really thrilling for Daudi and myself.'

'Words of truth,' broke in my assistant. 'They were, for as the tumour came out you could see the side of his face coming back into place. The twists disappeared, the mouth straightened and the eye, *yoh*, it was suddenly normal.'

Nusu laughed. 'But, Bwana, how I rejoiced when you asked for a mirror to be brought.'

Wendwa smiled. 'It was one of the things I will never forget, that moment when you first looked into that mirror.'

Nusu shook his head. 'It was quite beyond wonder. My tongue could grasp no words but my heart sang with joy. Bwana, no one could have done more for anyone than you have done for me. You have made my crooked places straight again. *Eeeh*!

'You showed me the small lump of stuff that was the cause of all the trouble. It was a worthless small thing. *Kah*! I rejoiced when I saw it go into the rubbish bin.'

'Suppose, Nusu, that we'd left that bandage over your face. It would have hidden your trouble. No one would have noticed and everyone would have said how neat the bandage looked.'

'But, you would not have removed the cause. My trouble would have remained. Also, to use both eyes and all your mouth is much better than only half.' He smiled an almost straight smile. 'You explained this to me carefully and simply. You said that it was this

173

swelling that made my face crooked, that made my life miserable and that made me frightened. You told me sin was like this, for sin twists, brings fear and misery and death.

'*Kumbe*, I understood. It was no good covering sin up. I had to come to the only One who could help to get rid of it. He is Jesus Christ, the Son of God.'

Daudi smiled. 'Jesus certainly took from your heart the sin that damages and twists. He forgave you. Behold, it was small hardship to the Bwana, nor did it cause him pain to remove your trouble. For Jesus it was altogether different and this is what God says about it, "Although he was the Son of God and equal with God, he put aside his divine glory and became human like you and me and lived humbly and appeared as a man amongst men. He was so obedient to God that he went to the point of giving up his life by dying like a criminal on the cross." And he did all this so that you and I might get rid of the twisting of sin from our lives.'

'*Kah*,' said Nusu. 'My life is different now, Bwana. People can look at me without shuddering and I have no shame and sorrow in my heart.'

Wistfully Goha looked across at me and said, 'Hope grows within me.'

Jungle Doctor Series

Jungle Doctor and the Whirlwind
ISBN 978-1-84550-296-6

Jungle Doctor on the Hop
ISBN 978-1-84550-297-3

Jungle Doctor Spots a Leopard
ISBN 978-1-84550-301-7

Jungle Doctor's Crooked Dealings
ISBN 978-1-84550-299-7

Jungle Doctor in Slippery Places
ISBN 978-1-84550-298-0

CHRISTIAN FOCUS PUBLICATIONS

Christian Focus | Christian Heritage | CF4K | Mentor

Christian Focus Publications publishes books for adults and children under its four main imprints: Christian Focus, CF4K, Mentor and Christian Heritage. Our books reflect that God's word is reliable and Jesus is the way to know him, and live for ever with him.

Our children's publication list includes a Sunday School curriculum that covers pre-school to early teens; puzzle and activity books. We also publish personal and family devotional titles, biographies and inspirational stories that children will love.

If you are looking for quality Bible teaching for children then we have an excellent range of Bible story and age specific theological books.

From pre-school to teenage fiction, we have it covered!

Find us at our web page:
www.christianfocus.com

CF4•K
Because you're never too young to know Jesus